Leveraging the Cloud Marketplace

— To —

Mitigate Risks, Costs and Complexities

Edward Mahon

Cloudworks Publishing Company

For information about permission to reproduce selections from this book, email cloudworks@edwardmahon.com.

Published by Cloudworks Publishing Company
Ponte Vedra, Florida

First printing: April 2019

ISBN 978-0-578-44405-5

Chapter Summary and Purpose

Chapter / Title	Chapter Purpose
Introduction	Why read this book?
	For whom this book is written
Chapter 1: The Cloud Value Proposition, including its Challenges	Linking business technology issues with the cloud's ability to help
Chapter 2: No Cloud Strategy, No IT Strategy	Building a cloud transition strategy
Chapter 3: Understanding Cloud Giants' Products	Reviewing four cloud giants' product lines
Chapter 4: Understanding the Cloud Marketplace	Reviewing the vendor marketplace structure
Chapter 5: Cloud Solutions	10 cloud use case criteria
Appendix: Activity Based Costing Tables	Assessing current costs

Table of Contents

INTRODUCTION

Chapter Outline

- Why read this book
- For whom the book is written

Why Read This Book

Who in their right mind starts a project that will likely last ten years, and during this period of time, increase risks, costs and complexities?

Transitioning Information Technology development and operations to the cloud *is* such a project. Given the task has these alarming attributes, let's hope the board of directors and the C-suite are patient!

While this book is a cloud proponent, if, in addition to increasing risks, costs and complexities, during the transition, you need additional justification not to move to cloud-delivered services, here are a few:

- The cloud vendor marketplace is in flux.
- There is a lack of uniform use of open standards and protocols.
- Vendor lock-in is likely.
- Project failure is a strong possibility.

If risks, costs and complexities are larger during a cloud transition, then delivering value along the way will be key. To be sure, over time, the disruptions will be replaced with business model improvements in the form of increased competitiveness and reduced costs. The cloud service delivery model will also be more manageable and predictable.

The Cloud is a Disruptive Trifecta	
Risk	Entering the cloud while it is significantly contracting & expanding with vendor business viability models failing regularly
Cost	Concurrently accruing operational expenses in both the premise-based data center and the cloud
Complexity	Requires the integration of legacy and cloud technology

Over the past several decades, how often has a new information technology been announced as a game changer, only to fail? Well, regarding the cloud, this time it's for real—both from a tactical and a strategic perspective.

As of the beginning of 2019, cloud-related expenditures exceed $600B a year and continue to grow. It is clear the cloud is a viable information technology service delivery model.

Whether you are driven by capturing cloud-related revenue (i.e., channel reseller), or you wish to reduce the cost of a cloud transition (i.e., chief information officer), this book will help. This book takes a comprehensive and multi-dimensional view of the cloud giants and the surrounding cloud marketplace.

Regardless, if you are an entrepreneur, an established C-level officer, or a product marketer, this book provides valuable information by drawing a relationship between business-related issues and cloud solutions that help.

If you support information technology operations and innovations, have a financial stake in corporate information technology costs, or are responsible for the company vision, products and services, you can't afford to ignore cloud-related decisions.

Regardless of the interest in the cloud, understanding the cloud giants and the surrounding marketplace will be necessary to drive revenue and value from the cloud.

Imagine a world in which you:

- Innovate and automate more quickly, reducing product and service time to market
- Get closer to your customers by developing a deeper understanding of their sentiment
- Use staff more strategically
- Reduce operational costs
- Improve integration with all business-related touch points
- Improve agility and scalability that directly translate to an improved return on investment

Sounds good, but these potential benefits come at a price.

Adopting the cloud as an entirely new service delivery model is very disruptive. To date, transitions have not been an easy ride. Worse yet, the transition will require attention to manage unavoidable changes to corporate processes, staff skills, and most of the underlying technology.

The cloud has emerged as the superior delivery option; however, it will be necessary to understand both the cloud giants' products and the surrounding vendor marketplace solutions.
Minimizing risks, costs and complexities during a cloud transition is a central theme throughout this book. In order to help manage these forces, I, the author, seek to help you, the reader, to gain a better understanding of the cloud's key components.

This book is written for the C-suite, and it reviews and contrasts cloud giants' (Amazon, Microsoft, Google, IBM, Salesforce, and Workday) products and services. It also includes a review of the surrounding partner marketplace structure for size, industry sector, technology and consulting services. The book also provides criteria associated with 10 different potential use cases that will help you weigh your options and formulate a plan. The use case criteria with help develop winning practices to leverage the cloud. The criteria help outline the transition challenges and highlight best practices. There is a high likelihood that one or more of the 10 use cases addresses a problem meaningful to you.

If you are a CIO and considering not moving to the cloud, consider the likely consequences. Your key customers, sister departments and suppliers may bypass you and move to the cloud themselves. If this happens, the result will be a disjointed set of solutions rather than an integrated and secure information technology architecture.

Furthermore, not embracing the cloud will limit your choices, moving forward. An indicator of this is understanding that all software built today is designed to run in the cloud.

The cloud is a fundamental change in how business information technology is developed, deployed and maintained, though the time to value varies significantly. Startup companies have adopted the cloud without hesitation, but established companies continue to struggle with the development of a cloud transition approach.

For Whom the Book Is Written

If you are a <u>Chief Information Officer</u> (CIO), you know transitioning to the cloud is a very large and risky project. Though your cloud strategy may be part of your reference architecture, you may still continue to struggle to assess how the cloud actually fits into the larger corporate business model. Further, it is a daunting task to assess the cloud marketplace for vendors that are a good fit. Additionally, reducing operational costs during the cloud transition will be difficult, especially if you have adopted a 'cloud first' mindset. Expenses will continue to grow in both the private data center and in the cloud.

This book may be able to help the CIO change his or her role to that of a cloud broker, serving all corporate departments, suppliers, and customers. Developing a cloud-managed service adds to the CIO's portfolio. This book can also assist the CIO with cloud vendor selection, vendor contracts, and service level agreements as it assists with a cloud implementation for all corporate departments. A cloud broker strategy will help the CIO to avoid being left behind.

If you make a living as a <u>Channel Reseller or Cloud Solution Company</u> selling information technology products and services, then you know how difficult it is to sell into an environment that puts the purchaser at risk and will likely not reach a positive return on investment for an extended period of time. Selling into a marketplace that is constantly contracting and expanding is difficult. In order to help customers know how to dampen risks and complexity, you clearly will want to understand the cloud marketplace.

If you are a <u>Chief Financial Officer</u> or otherwise responsible for balancing the books and addressing business challenges, then a few items of concern exist:

- Controlling the change from a capital intensive (CapEx) model to the cloud's operating cost (OpEx) subscription schema.

- Living in two worlds (private data center and the cloud) will increase cost. Transitioning an entire information technology operation from a privately-owned platform to a shared public model is a significant challenge and change in culture. For the average size data center operation, the transition will take 5 to 10 years. At a minimum, it certainly is a multiyear endeavor, and the size and difficulty continue to grow each day. It is difficult to estimate the percentage of corporate IT data centers that will have moved entirely to the cloud during the next few years; however, yours is likely one of them. At a time when businesses must cut costs, the cloud will actually increase them until all operations reside in the cloud.

- The rate of cloud spending increases are already outpacing that of any other category of the IT budget! So, monitoring the expenditures and spending wisely makes sense!

- Regardless of how the cloud adoption occurs, things are going to become more complex and subsequently riskier. And these increases will exist until the transition is complete.

If you are a <u>Chief Executive Officer</u> or otherwise set strategic direction, then developing a strong sense of the cloud's true value and direction will help you make informed decisions and improve your management team's visibility. Assessing potential cloud partners that can help sell products and services will assist in setting a competitive differentiation. Knowledge of the cloud's strategic value will help ensure the executive team and CIO maintain an application-centric perspective (one that will produce corporate value more quickly).

Targeted Sections of This Book

	Chapter 1	Chapter 2	Chapter 3	Chapter 4	Chapter 5
Chief Information Officer	✓	✓	✓	✓	✓
Chief Financial Officer	✓	✓		✓	✓
Chief Executive Officer	✓	✓		✓	✓
Chief Information Security Officer	✓	✓	✓	✓	✓
Chief Procurement Officer	✓	✓		✓	✓
Chief Marketing Officer	✓			✓	✓
Chief Human Talent Officer	✓	✓		✓	✓
Government & Commercial Reseller	✓		✓		✓
Cloud Technology Partners	✓			✓	✓
Cloud Solutions Companies	✓		✓	✓	
Chief Cloud Architect	✓	✓	✓		✓
Vice President Of Infrastructure	✓	✓	✓	✓	✓
Product Positioning Officer	✓		✓	✓	✓
Line Of Business Officers	✓			✓	✓
Channel Resellers	✓			✓	✓

Key Cloud Attributes and Categories

a. Cloud Infrastructure, management tools, and utilities
  i. Compute Platform, including serverless and high-performance computing
  ii. Storage solutions
  iii. Content Delivery Network, including data acceleration tools, software-defined networking, load balancing and caching services
  iv. Security, Compliance and Identity Management Service
  v. Migration tools, planning, architecting and building
  vi. Management tools
  vii. Business continuity (disaster recovery, archiving, backup and restore)
  viii. Monitoring in a hybrid world
  ix. Provisioning and automating the stack
  x. Cloud pricing tools

b. Data Management and Analytics
  i. Databases
  ii. Business Intelligence, warehouses, big data, analytic tools, mining unstructured and structured data
  iii. Master data platforms

c. Application Services
  i. Application development tools, including mobile development platforms, tools, and services
  ii. Machine Learning/Artificial Intelligence
  iii. Internet of Things
  iv. Media Services
  v. Integration (API connectors)
  vi. Automating/streamlining business & workload processes
  vii. E-commerce & Websites
  viii. Email, messaging, and collaboration
  ix. Content Management
  x. ERP
  xi. CRM
  xii. Gaming

CHAPTER 1
The Cloud Value Proposition, Including Its Challenges

Chapter Outline

- Chapter introduction: Business productivity benefits
- A brief cloud definition
- Outlining the cloud transition challenges
- What to expect from the cloud, if managed correctly
  - The opportunity to completely redesign the information infrastructure
  - Quicken time to value
  - The ability to retain the value of sunk software investments
  - A development platform that provides an integrated and life cycle approach to managing application deployment

- o The need to loosen control and trust your cloud provider
- o Streamlining processes, tasks, self-service interfaces, and provisioning
- o Resource usage improvement
- o Enabling real-time scalability
- o An improved environment that attracts and retains the brightest staff
- o The opportunity to ensure your infrastructure is continuously refreshed
- o Living in both worlds for many years to come
- o Switching from a CapEx to OpEx model
- o Minimizing disruption
- o Vendor lock-in
- What not to expect from the cloud, anytime soon:
  - o A short transition
  - o Reduced risk
  - o Building an entrance strategy without an exit strategy
  - o Reduced complexity
  - o Reduced costs
  - o Immediately innovate

Chapter Introduction:
Business Productivity Benefits

These days, technology is getting closer to business objectives. To assist, the cloud has been designed to enable quicker deployment periods, normalize annual capital expenditures, and to ensure your data and applications are protected and always available. The cloud can be faster, cheaper, and more scalable than your current privately-owned data center environment. But only over time and only if you tend to it.

In fact, many IT functions, such as mining unstructured data or effectively building and managing mobile applications, are not possible without the use of the cloud. Hence, leveraging the cloud provides an unprecedented opportunity to transform IT and improve its value.

The cloud has proven itself and is worthy of the most important parts of your company's information infrastructure. The cloud is where the most important information technology innovations are occurring. This is true regardless if it is a simple email, a full-blown ERP, software operation and development environment, or primary storage repositories.

Why not use the cloud transition as a catalyst to develop business advantages, such as:

- Assess software development tools for consistency, obsolescence, cost and capability

- Begin provisioning with container and orchestration technology

- Build a reference architecture

- Improve integration between dissimilar systems

- Strengthen security

- Increase the use of data standards and open source approaches

- Develop a simpler and more consistent environment

Given the complexities associated with the types of ideas mentioned above, it makes sense to carefully assess where and how to gain value from the cloud. Fiscal management goals should be to remove redundancies, reduce unused capacity, and ultimately reduce costs.

For any company looking to get the most out of their IT infrastructure investments, the cloud is likely a good fit.

If you are a startup company, the cloud is a good match. Often, startup companies have a culture that can better handle disruption than that of established companies. Instead of startups investing capital to build a data center, they see the merit of a cloud OpEx model. This allows the repurposing of those capital dollars to other necessary expenditures. Also, as startups know, variable OpEx expenditures are easier to manage. If you are an established company, you might value moving away from operating a data center as it likely consumes a great deal of staff time and attention.

Of all the reasons to consider the cloud, better staff utilization is far and away the most important benefit. Why not consider the cloud as a means of better utilizing your IT staff? Worthy of consideration is a model that combines their intellectual capital, ability to innovate and deploy software applications more quickly.

The challenge to the information technology staff during a cloud transition is doubled as they must maintain legacy expertise (i.e., running the data center or maintaining existing software applications) while also learning new cloud technology. The cloud will require staff roles and information technology departments to develop or augment skills such as:

- Business savvy experts that spend time learning customer needs
- Cost accountants, not just IT budgeteers
- Vendor relationship experts
- Contract and service level agreement (SLA) specialists

A Brief Cloud Definition

Think of the cloud as a facilitator of transactions. Leveraging the internet, customers can access services from anywhere. The cloud can be public (often referred to as a multi-tenant environment), private, or a mix of the two.

At its core, the cloud is a collection of networked devices able to provide compute and storage services, contained in cloud data centers across the globe.

Think of cloud selections as outsourcing much of the data center hardware and software. In doing so, unlike a privately-owned data center, much of the maintenance actions are handled by the cloud provider. However, the amount and type of customer maintenance efforts vary significantly, as reflected directly below and in more detail in Chapter 3. Similar to the national power grid and utility network, the cloud has an automated scaling capacity with pay for only what you use pricing models.

While several new service delivery models or fulfillment methods have cropped up, the original three are:

Infrastructure as a Service (IaaS)

The cloud provider owns and manages the lower layers of the stack while providing compute capabilities, storage capacity, network access, security and a host of infrastructure tools to help manage the migration and ongoing operation.

Platform as a Service (PaaS)

Enables the user to develop and manage applications without also the need to maintain the balance of the infrastructure. Important elements of a PaaS environment include programming tools, mobile development capability, and multi-cloud integration features.

Software as a Service (SaaS)

Offered here are software packages in which the selected cloud provider runs nearly all aspects of the operation. SaaS application revisions are constantly updated, usually without customer related duties.

Outlining Cloud Transition Challenges

Migrating to the cloud can enhance service, quicken application delivery, improve resiliency, help analyze consumer spending patterns, and lower costs. However, the cloud has difficulties, too. Simply said, the cloud currently has too many moving parts. To name a few:

- Cloud marketplace vendors are constantly coming and going, making vendor choices difficult.

- Legacy technology providers are finding it difficult to pivot to the cloud.

- Legacy software licensing models are giving way to subscription-based service, which burdens existing budget models.

- The quick rate new cloud vendor products are arriving results in difficulty evaluating them.

- Emerging technologies are testing existing operations. Implementing these changes has a high value but requires detailed planning. Examples of new technologies that require thoughtful planning include:

  o New real-time replication software and data storage techniques, regardless of the application, require complete architectural redesigns (i.e., archival, traditional backup and recovery, business continuity & disaster recovery).

  o Improving provisioning capability via new containerization technology (as opposed to many current premise-based virtualized environments).

  o Leveraging new API hubs and connectors to better integrate data and their applications.

Adding to these challenges, are the usual suspects to manage in the workplace, consisting of people, processes, time and money. The cloud adds yet another layer. Over time, the cloud will need to evolve into a simpler environment and one that is easier to integrate and manage. Further adding to the cloud transition complexity, is the integration between cloud technology and premise-based legacy architectures.

When assessing the cloud, be mindful of operating principles such as:

- Maintaining focus on desired business outcomes.
- Developing a plan of how to manage a culture of change.
- Learning and following changes in the cloud marketplace.
- Assessing changes to the underlying cloud technology.
- Paying close attention to your cloud vendor's sustainability.
- Using an cost accounting system to assess legacy environments for costs, staff activities and areas to improve.
- Developing a cloud transition plan.
- Making the correct staff talent and skill acquisitions.

What to Expect from the Cloud, if Managed Correctly

The Opportunity to Completely Redesign the Information Infrastructure

Do you recall the phrase, "never waste a good budget crisis to invoke change not otherwise possible without the crises?" What makes this management technique ring true, is sometimes it takes a new and large catalyst to enable fundamental change to occur.

Why not use the same mindset to re-architect the entire information infrastructure when migrating to the cloud? Use the cloud as the catalyst to drive the design of a new reference architecture.

You could implement most of the new methodologies and solutions mentioned in the book without the cloud, but you haven't yet! Why is that? Maybe a fundamental change in IT delivery is needed. When will an opportunity arise again that can enable a complete architectural redesign?

Upon review of your existing architecture, you will find many existing workloads and infrastructure components should be upgraded, replaced or retired, enabling the repurpose of significant staff time and other expenses.

Huge staff opportunity costs are wrapped up in maintaining older software. The time could be spent improving the innovation process (i.e., striving to better understand customer preferences with new cloud machine learning processes). Or the staff could be freed to build new revenue generating software applications.

By leveraging the cloud's new tools, services, and products, the result could be a state-of-the-art technology environment. The current information infrastructure can be replaced or improved.

Also, while you are at it, why not leverage the movement to the cloud as a means to conduct good old fashion housekeeping? For example, before moving data to the cloud, consider revisiting data retention policies. Are the current retention policies adhered to, or is every bit of the data generated also retained, making it impossible to continue to store and backup enormous amounts of data?

Quicken Time to Value

It is hard to over-emphasize this suggestion, as it is the most important outcome resulting from investments in information technology. Getting products and services to market enables new revenue streams.

The Ability to Retain Value from Sunk Software Investments

In many cases, the cloud giants and the legacy software companies allow for software previously purchased perpetual license to also run in the cloud at no additional cost. This has high-cost avoidance, as it is one less necessary change, reducing both staff time spent on the task and user disruption.

A Development Platform that Provides an Integrated and Life Cycle Approach to Managing Application Deployment

With the use of new software development platforms and tools (i.e., Salesforce's force.com), the development process is quick. Using one platform can also help to develop consistent life cycles across all applications.

The Need to Loosen Control and Trust Your Cloud Providers

Committing to a vendor or set of vendors is a significant change when selecting the cloud as a new service delivery model. Today, much, if not all, of the data center is completely under the CIO's control. Routine, though very important duties such as protecting data and production operations (i.e., routine backup and recovery) are completely the responsibility of the CIO. In the cloud, functions like these are likely completely out of the CIO's control. While there are ways to stay closely coupled to operations (with the use of service level agreements) using the cloud (i.e., SaaS offerings), it does require trusting the cloud vendor to run operations properly.

Streamlining Processes, Tasks, Self-Service Interfaces and Provisioning

Why not implement complete, automated and standardized self-service processes and provisioning workload models in the cloud? Thoughts for consideration:

- Are your processes and self-service interfaces user friendly and intuitive to use?

- Do they require a human to manually field and address customer requests?

- How integrated are all of the processes?

- Do all of the processes have the same look and feel to the customer?

Likely a new cloud-based workflow design will improve things.

Think of automation in terms of:

- Information access; customer self-service
- Workflow and processes
- Provisioning staff intensive operational tasks

And, oh yeah, don't pave the cow path! Meaning, before moving current workloads to the cloud, consider the value of conducting a needs assessment and process analysis. The goal to improve and simplify the business processes, resulting in a more flexible, adaptable and scalable set of workloads. This should rank high on the list of value received from IT investments and the movement to the cloud.

Let's face it, all industries strive to better understand their customers, and regardless of which industry sector, most processes were designed to serve the customer. In order to drive down costs and positively impact revenue, process improvements should be made regularly. These workloads likely need to be streamlined, more innovative and easier to use. But this type of change is difficult as the processes often weave through the entire corporation with ownership resting with departments outside the Information Technology unit.

What if you were able to deliver additional revenue generating applications faster to market? To improve agility as a result of redesigning existing processes. And do so while developing the tools necessary to continuously improve future application development processes?

Resource Usage Improvement

Capacity Utilization

Reducing unused capacity speaks to removing costs that add no value, as it is the most expensive cost in the information technology budget. Most organizations underutilize their servers and storage devices. Further, most are uncertain of their actual capacity requirements.

Typically, premise-based systems buying practices procure more storage and compute capacity than is needed, either to ensure peak usage requirements can be met or to provide growth capability.

A footnote here regarding cloud pricing models: There is an irony at play when selecting reserved pricing in the cloud, as it often results in unused capacity as well. It requires one to estimate future capacity needs, just as is the case with premise-based procurement! This is not something most IT managers are good at! There are other cloud pricing models to choose from, such as spot pricing; however, their unit cost is higher. By the way, as indicated in Chapter 2, I make reference to the need for a cost accountant. Such a skill is needed when making pricing model decisions to best meet current and future capacity needs in the cloud.

Time Utilization

Often parts of the private data center lay idle as much as 120 hours a week or three-quarters of the time in a given week. Yet, because you own the equipment, you are paying infrastructure costs regardless of whether it is in use. In the cloud, you pay only when you are using the computing and storage cycles.

Enabling Real-Time Scalability

Real-time scalability provides the ability to add capacity as needed during peak usage periods, and it is a wonderful design concept that solves an important problem. For example, if a web site experiences unexpected traffic increases, it can handle it. This is the case regardless of whether the web application lives in a hybrid cloud (i.e., part of the application lives in the private data center and part in the cloud). However, designing and configuring a design to accomplish this function will likely require your staff to learn new skills.

An Improved Environment that Attracts and Retains the Brightest Staff

The best staff highly value designing and working in a well thought out and innovative environment. Not only will such an environment attract highly qualified individuals, but by freeing them from low-level duties, as the cloud enables, increases their value to the company. For example, what if they were able to gain greater insight into how the company runs and how a new software development process in the cloud can help increase profits and reduce expenses? The list of benefits of more productive staff is endless. In fact, it is likely the most important value of all.

The Opportunity to Ensure Your Infrastructure Is Continuously Refreshed

The use of the cloud changes the traditional vendor/customer relationship in key ways. The cloud provider now assumes the R&D effort and expense to maintain key areas of the infrastructure. This reduces customer overhead headaches.

Living in Both Worlds for Many Years to Come

Most established companies run their own data centers as well as subscribing to select cloud services. This will further complicate the overall information infrastructure; however, very few options exist. Companies will live in this hybrid world for many years to come.

Switching from a CapEx to OpEx Model

Most budget methodologies are designed around the need to depreciate capital expenditures over the life of a purchased asset. This helps normalize one-time capital expenses during a given year (i.e., developing a plant fund as a savings account). However, the cloud is an equipment lease model which removes the one-time equipment purchases but likely raises the monthly operating costs. The adjustment period is made more difficult during the cloud transition as both the private data center and cloud expenses occur, raising the overall cost of operations.

Minimizing Disruption

Much of the cloud transition will be disruptive. Assessing value, effort, cost, and level of disruption will be important. For example, moving Microsoft Exchange email to the cloud is not intrusive to the user, and the cloud marketplace has many experienced vendors to assist with an email migration. On the other hand, changing business software, such as an ERP or a database, will be very disruptive.

Vendor Lock-In

Very few, if any, transitions will not result in a vendor lock-in scenario. Simply said, the cost and effort to move data, build an application or port an existing one to the cloud is non-trivial. The interest or desire to then undo the effort to move to another cloud provider will be small, to say the least.

What Not to Expect from the Cloud, Anytime Soon

Though there are numerous reasons and merit in considering a cloud transition, let's have a reality check. Below are six items not to expect.

A Short Transition

Change is often difficult. Change often meets with resistance. Remember the old phrase, "we hate our systems until it is time to give them up, then we love them." And if the change is truly transformational, it will take time. Good old fashion project management will be necessary, with the usual suspects, such as:

- Look for short-term wins.
- Let the customer own and drive the pace and nature of the change.
- Over-communicate, over-communicate.
- Obtain ownership from the key stakeholders.
- Don't allow the transition to be viewed as a technology project.

Reduced Risk

Living in two worlds is more difficult and risky than living in one (i.e., cloud and premise data center). For example, expanding and maintaining an identity management system that serves both environments during the transition will be more difficult and risky. The project itself is also risky, as key elements may fail. It is difficult to deliver large-scale projects on time and on budget, regardless of their purpose or type.

Building an Entrance Strategy Without an Exit Strategy

Building a cloud entrance strategy is difficult, but concurrently building an exit strategy doubles the complexity. However, it is a requirement. At a moment's notice, you may need to change cloud providers. Special care will be needed to ensure data and application portability are built into the exit strategy.

Reduced Complexity

Operational complexity will become more difficult—at least until the cloud transition is complete. Duties such as managing more contracts, more complex architecture, and additional vendor relationships will increase complexity.

Reduced Costs

Reducing the data center footprint is valuable though indirect overhead costs will not decrease proportionally as functions are moved to the cloud. Further, the cloud operational expenses will begin to accrue as you move infrastructure to the cloud. The cloud will not produce cost advantages until the entire premise-based data center costs are stopped. Until you complete the cloud transition, your costs actually go up.

Immediately Innovate

Much of the cloud focuses on operations, not application development, and for good reason. Getting to the point of using the tools that help innovate will not come until you have the operational infrastructure in place (i.e., on/off ramp to the cloud). The timeline to better innovate is extended further as training staff with the new development platform will be time-consuming.

CHAPTER 2
Business Impact While Transitioning to the Cloud

Chapter Outline

- Chapter Introduction
  - Business impact while improving business outcomes
  - Building a roadmap to the cloud
- Key factors influencing cloud adoption
  - Documenting the current environment
  - Cloud planning action items
  - Questions to inform the strategy
  - Decision points and their trade offs
  - Outsourcing and service level agreements
    - Is the cloud outsourcing?
    - Why outsource?
    - Service level agreements (SLA) and their value

- - Typical elements of the SLA
  - New SLAs concepts used in the cloud
- Methods of cloud adoption:
  - Design principles and considerations
  - Cloud related strategic goals: speed is paramount
  - Preparatory, transition and deployment actions
    - Conduct a needs assessment
    - Analyze the data
    - Develop a cost management system to assess cloud provider pricing differences
    - Cloud pricing

Chapter Introduction

Business Impact While Improving Business Outcomes

Businesses today have embraced the cloud to a very high degree. Cloud computing has become a key competitive advantage for all industry sectors from consumer discretionary to consumer staples to energy to financials to utilities to transportation to defense to health care. The list goes on.

However, no longer can a few low-risk, small steps to the cloud be considered a wise cloud strategy. Instead, the action necessary is to develop a plan to fully transition to the cloud.

The challenge when building a cloud strategy is the need to both learn the cloud's piece parts, including its major actors, while concurrently documenting your current environment.

In order to address necessary transition-related actions, this chapter provides questions that, when answered, result in a thorough understanding of the current environment. To assist, this chapter also provides a host of action items to consider while conducting the assessment. As all significant challenges require due diligence, the chapter then outlines critical trade-off criteria to consider. In fact, the transition to the cloud is all about trade-offs. They center around contrasting value vs. risk, complexity and cost. Identifying these factors is one of the book's primary themes. The goal is to become grounded in the characteristics of your current environment.

The plan should determine which steps into the cloud can produce transformational business value while also ensuring how to completely transition to the cloud. That is, which steps will accelerate the pace of innovation and obtain the quickest value while also enabling a move to the cloud.

This chapter highlights the type of data needed regarding your current operation. The chapter also suggests current issues and problems to solve in order to drive more value from your IT investments regardless of the service delivery model.

Building a Roadmap to the Cloud

Plan of attack to create a cloud transition strategy:

- Conduct a needs assessment
- Formulate the questions to inform the strategy
- Identify the trade-offs to weigh
- Develop the design principles and considerations to build the plan

So, a cloud strategy is needed. Contrasting the cloud and your issues requires attention to detail and can take time. However, don't create a lengthy strategy, as things are changing quickly. Key elements can become dated quickly. The actual challenge is to determine how to orchestrate the transition. The key will be to develop a structured approach that is project-oriented and use case specific.

The goal will be to develop secure and innovative solutions that increase customer and shareholder value. You must drive your digital business with flexible, highly scalable, elastic and low-cost solutions.

It is likely you have moved some items to the cloud already, and you have leveraged portions of the cloud as needed. A hybrid cloud has resulted from migrating applications to both private and public clouds. A process such as this can result in an evolution that is a disjointed infrastructure between the premise-based data center and those new applications in the cloud. In most cases, there is little choice. The architecture will remain a hybrid environment until the entire premise-based data center is shut down.

Cloud Transition 'To Do' List:

- Assess current information infrastructure for cost, obsolescence and value

- Document current and future priorities (infrastructure and applications)

- Learn the cloud giants' products and services, including how to leverage its marketplace vendors

- Review cloud use cases

- Develop your unique road map to the cloud

Key Factors Influencing Cloud Adoption

Documenting the Current Environment

Before contrasting cloud-related characteristics to that of the current environment, it is important to document all aspects of the current operation. Doing so will result in a foundation that will help smooth the journey to the cloud. Consider using the inventory planning tables located in the appendix of this book.

The cloud assessment goal is to determine if a cloud-enabled environment, when complete, will enable increased innovation and potentially provide a reduction in costs. The opportunity to gain operational improvements and agility has proven to be worth the effort.

The planning exercise should include as much of the staff as possible. Therefore, ensure you have a process of inclusion with them every step of the way.

Questions to Inform the Strategy

- Do you have a plan to completely integrate your premise data center and the cloud during the transition? What efforts are necessary to integrate multiple applications?

- Does the plan conclude with completely turning off all legacy data center operations?

- Does the cloud strategy address all critical issues?

- Has the strategy adopted a 'cloud first' requirement for all new project activity?

- Which cloud transition actions will drive the most value in the shortest period of time?

- How quickly can a cloud on/off ramp from your current data center to the cloud be built while concurrently adopting an application-centric focus?

- Will the cloud provide improved value to the corporate mission? If so, how?

- Does the cloud reduce costs? If so, how and over what length of time?

- Is your current IT infrastructure dated? If so, repurposing the funds needed to update the current environment can help fund a cloud transition.

- How can the cloud adoption strategy be less disruptive?

- How can the cloud migration be simplified?

- Do the corporate processes and workflows need improvement?

- Are modern orchestration, provisioning and automation technologies currently used in the IT operation?

- What percentage of staff are engaged in developing innovative solutions or customer-facing activities vs. back office operational duties?

- Is the right IT talent and its management in place?

- How will cloud vendors be selected and sourced?

- Can the IT department become a cloud broker for all other corporate units?

- Can the cloud help better protect company data? If so, how?

- Are you able to focus on improving the use of open standard protocols?

Decision Points and Their Trade-Offs

Good news. Waiting to fully move to the cloud has reduced risk and has provided more clarity. The cloud marketplace has been fragmented and has had inevitable vendor failures by those that did not have sustainable business models. The use of standardized tools is now available and used much in the same way across different cloud service providers.

Moving forward, consider framing trade-off decisions around risk, disruption levels, potential value, complexity, available funding and staff opportunity costs. Discuss with key stakeholders the relationship implications such as:

- Implications of not entering the cloud

- Risk of project failure

- Project costs

- Innovation vs. disruption tolerance

If a company has not yet initiated any cloud projects, an argument could be made that the risks were too high. However, risks exist regardless of if entering the cloud or not.

There is no downside or risk to getting on with creating the underpin connections between the cloud and the data center. This work consists of items such as creating cloud network connections, compute instances, storage configurations, integrating identity management systems and numerous other common security practices.

No two cloud transitions are the same; however, all have common elements. Sooner or later though, it will be necessary to use the cloud to deliver the most critical solutions, regardless if building into a SaaS environment, completely re-architect applications, or simply rehosting existing applications to the cloud.

The opportunity to extend partnerships with and between business executives also exists when moving to the cloud. Large-scale projects that reduce costs and sell more product are unifying. Arguments will be minimized with outcomes that truly increase innovation and flexibility.

Cloud Planning Action Items

- Contrast cloud products and services
- Build a multi-cloud vendor adoption model that includes a clear integration strategy
- Develop a reference architecture that provides clear guideposts during the transition
- Develop cloud use cases unique to your environment
- Develop new self-service provisioning techniques
- Re-orchestrate and configure standard workload practices and processes
- Review current data standards
- Assess installed storage solutions
- Evaluate current development model
- Appropriately staff an effort to learn the cloud's new subscription-based pricing models while preparing a model to move to it
- Assess how the cloud is changing so you can move with it (expenses, technology, potential value, needed skills)
- Assess where process efficiencies and staff productivity can occur

Outsourcing and Service-Level Agreements

Is the Cloud Outsourcing?

Simply said, outsourcing involves assigning specific activities to another company to manage. With the use of a binding contract, outsourcing generally involves transferring daily decisions and operations to another company. Sounds like the cloud is outsourcing.

Why Outsource?

- Improve service: The vendor can do a specific service better and possibly more effectively. Results can improve customer satisfaction through increased performance.

- Reduce staff opportunity cost: Outsourcing a particular function improves employee value as it enables those staff members to concentrate on other, likely more strategic, activities.

- Reduce operating and/or capital costs.

Service Level Agreements (SLA) and Their Value

Management and control have always been a part of business endeavors, and SLAs have been used since the beginning of contractual agreements. And for good reason, as they help avoid misunderstandings and manage expectations between those bound by the contract. They allow all parties to translate their objectives into contractual language. SLAs provide for the assurance of agreed upon contract commitments. SLAs define requirements, scope of services and performance standards. Because a cloud vendor exit strategy is very difficult, SLAs take on heightened importance.

An implied backdrop to any contract is the need to ensure the chosen vendor has the incentive to innovate and remain viable. Key components of the SLA include the ability to measure performance and to review the value derived from the contract (remember the phrase: that which gets measured, gets managed). The SLA must describe what the service or software will do functionally and how well will it do it.

Typical Elements of a Traditional SLA

- Pricing schedules that include limits on price increases
- Reliability guarantees (continuity of service)
- Performance guarantees
- Credit provided if services fall below agreed-upon levels
- Access to provider audit results
- Agreed-upon down times during maintenance periods
- Payment terms
- Termination provisions
- Conflict resolution

Newer SLA Concepts Used in the Cloud

With the cloud, not only is the production of a service transferred, but so too are the underlying architectural decisions. The outsourced activities and assets can include baseline technology, facilities, technology gear, and people. Some cloud-related SLAs include:

- Data portability
- When requested, how quickly your data will be returned and in what format
- Requirement to destroy data remaining on vendor cloud system after contract termination
- Outline where data can and cannot reside
- Terms during the transition

Methods of Cloud Adoption

Design Principles and Considerations

Building a cloud transition strategy based on key and predefined elements increases the likelihood of meeting specific business needs for scale, operations, security, and compliance. As you drive the new digital transformation, consider organizing your cloud transition strategy in three parts:

- Strategic goals
- Preparatory actions
- Transition activities

Or, the goals and actions could also be indexed as:

- Vendor
- Technology
- Fiscal
- Policy
- Project implementation

The choices are straight forward:

1. **Lift and shift: Migrate and re-host applications and workloads as an IaaS solution.**

   That is, move the existing premise-based application to the cloud with little or no modifications. Simply spin up a cloud server instance, storage, network connection and move the workload to the cloud. The user will likely not know the application lives in a different location and as such this option is the least disruptive. The lift and shift option is also likely the lowest cost option to move legacy applications; however, it also does not offer enhancements otherwise found with newer applications.

Also, migrating the legacy application to a cloud-based IaaS platform will not relieve the staff of application maintenance or most system administration duties.

2. **Completely rewrite the application as a cloud native application.**

Move the users and start anew. Clearly the most expensive option and staff intensive but would result in improved functionality, if needed. If additional functionality is not needed, simply leave the workload on site and spend your efforts elsewhere.

3. **Replace it with a SaaS offering.**

Replacing a premise-based application with a SaaS offering would be chosen in order to derive more value. Functional enhancements can be obtained such as improved usability, better performance, obtain specific new functionality, streamline a current process, or develop stronger integrations with other applications.

If your functional needs can be met by a vendor-supported application, then an SaaS (Software as a Service) alternative is the best option. The SaaS option also allows your team to step away from the application's daily management duties and focus on other tasks. It will be the most disruptive option; however, it will likely have the most value.

4. **Leave the application in the data center and set an end of life date.**

Setting an end-of-life date for selected legacy applications while building or buying their replacements is a very good option. Replacing the legacy application with another that better meets future needs is a good choice. An equal benefit comes after the legacy application is actually decommissioned, as costs and complexity of running the older application are removed.

Choosing to remove applications from the IT portfolio is more valuable than deciding where it physically lives (i.e., premise data center or in the cloud). If end-of-life is set for an application, results include reduced staff support time, hardware and licensing reductions and likely an improved user interface.

Choices to host the application include more than a public multi-tenant infrastructure (i.e., shared virtualized cloud option). Though a public cloud is most often chosen, other combinations and choices include:

- Private cloud-like, on premise

- Private cloud, in the cloud

- Hosted environment in a private data center

Private clouds add costs and complexity. Given the public cloud giants have security measures equal to or better than premise-based data centers, don't bother with a private cloud. Further, private clouds introduce increased interoperability issues and complexity. Service level agreements can be put in place to ensure the performance meets expectations while operating in the public multi-tenant cloud.

Regardless of which option is chosen, stay focused on those functions the company values the most to generate revenue, reduce costs, learn customer sentiment and simple good old fashion customer service.

Cloud-Related Strategic Goals: Speed Is Paramount

- Business value analysis: First and always, assess all potential actions for their business value.

- The Chief Information Officer should develop a cloud broker mentality and an understanding of cloud capabilities and requirements. Strive to understand how to tune and optimize cloud systems to run enterprise applications at their highest levels.

- Create a cloud sourcing strategy.

- Change how IT delivery is conducted.

- Develop a cloud first; multi-cloud vendor strategy.

- Innovate, innovate, innovate.

- Seize the moment to re-architect the information infrastructure and create a reference architecture.

- Adopt an application-centric approach to the cloud and focus on those critical applications.

- Expand the security strategy to include the cloud. Good old fashion governance and data security techniques remain a requirement.

- Continuously make data and software integration pervasive.

Cloud integration platforms are very important as they facilitate data exchange and application synchronization. Applying standardization across API connectors, networks, master data, and multiple cloud vendors is critical. Successful enterprise architects will also need to address standardization. The use of standards simplifies and optimizes integration between dissimilar services. The use of built-in software connectors also has speeded up the integration process.

From an integration perspective, it will be tough, given the cloud strategy will likely include a multitude of cloud vendors, existing vendors, customers, and the premise infrastructure. The converged infrastructure will need to be addressed at several levels, including applications, APIs, data standardization and infrastructure.

Design components that will help with integration include:

- Paying attention to API management

- Teasing out master data

- Embracing open source standards

- Revisiting every component and layer in the stack

The cloud's evolution is making the digital transition more difficult and risky. As the digital transformation continues to mature, so too the cloud is evolving to support it. The cloud marketplace is an element of the cloud ecosystem that is evolving the most (companies with cloud products and services and have structured partner relationships with the cloud giants). However, many of these marketplace companies have not developed a sustainable business model. The cloud marketplace is outlined in Chapter 4.

To learn how the cloud is evolving, spend time in areas such as:

- How the industry is restructuring
- New cloud services
- New and existing companies creating partnerships
- Open container initiatives
- Assess and choose information technology vendors, current and future cloud providers.

Another important cloud transition decision is to recognize the value of creating solid cloud vendor partnerships. There is too much at stake not to have a complete understanding of both current and future vendor products. Both the cloud giants and their surrounding marketplace partners will help with items such as migrating data, assess your security strategy, tailor SaaS software applications and integrate applications and data.

As a sidebar, the opportunity is disappearing for technology vendors not positioned in the cloud.

Steps to assess and choose cloud vendors:

- Assess the value and costs of current IT vendors.
- Study the cloud giants and their marketplace vendor partners, including who has aligned with who.
- Choose vendors that understand the cloud and how they fit.
- Choose vendors that are willing to take the time to understand the IT strategy and overall business.
- Invest the time to develop or strengthen existing vendor partnerships.
- Assign or hire a vendor relationship manager.

Preparatory, Transition and Deployment Actions

Conduct a Needs Assessment

As a first step to prepare for the cloud, a complete understanding of the current IT portfolio is necessary. Build on what is known about the current IT portfolio. Take a look at the tables in the appendix of this book; possibly they can help assess your current environment. That is, learn the current IT portfolio for its value and critical issues. The current IT service delivery model likely has its own issues that require resolution prior to moving to the cloud, so assessing them up front is a good idea. Rightsizing your current infrastructure is a critical step in successfully moving to the cloud. Assessing the current environment is critical, in order to understand and prioritize its most pressing items and areas to improve. It is likely there are more issues within the current IT operation, than with the cloud.

Prior to entering the cloud, develop a set of preparation actions.

Typical Issues within the current operation include:

- Process duplication and inefficiencies
- Employee utilization is titled more to operations, not innovation
- Level of current vendor utilization is poor
- Inadequate future storage and compute capacity
- Age of current legacy infrastructure
- Performance needs and capability aren't known
- Too many under-utilized and unintegrated management tools
- Inability for current cost accounting system to incorporate cloud pricing models

Analyze the Data

Concerns exist with regard to data privacy and data residency. It is important to gain control and an understanding of the data (i.e., its type, volume, use, and life cycle). Often:

- Data consistency is poor
- It is unknown how much new data will be created
- How much capacity is needed
- Data growth is out of control. Remember all of this data needs to be processed and stored.
- Comprehensive data governance teams do not exist

Other Preparatory, Transition and Deployment Actions

- Data portability is important. Plan for the high likelihood a cloud vendor will consolidate with another cloud company or worst case; their business viability disappears.
- Rationalize current software applications for their value, usability, longevity, life cycle and cost of ownership.
- Assess the relationship between capacity and utilization for compute, memory and storage across all instances.
- Develop cloud transition champions with the departments served by the cloud.
- Learn from cloud use cases and success stories.
- Build a cloud implementation team to help minimize migration issues. Project management principles apply, that of engaging everyone, from stakeholders to IT staff to current vendors to selected cloud providers.
- Work hand-in-hand with the company legal department when procuring cloud services.
- Assess the merit of speeding up transformative changes. Consider pulling the band aid off more quickly, that is, use the big bang approach.
- Develop and routinely share widely a clear cloud migration plan.
- Develop an integrated monitoring and performance management platform.
- Assess the current level of customer self-service provisioning for:

- o   Automation
- o   Ease of use
- o   Ability to collect and analyze data
- o   Complexity and serviceability
- Independent of the cloud, find and develop orchestration tools to help with automation via standard provisioning tools to improve digital customer interaction.
- Update security policies and tools.
- Assess the way your company collects, analyzes, and distributes customer information.
- Assess the type of IT talent needed in the future. It will be important to offload staff of operational tasks, enabling the repurposing of their workload to that of more important business objectives. From the outset, it is important to manage the significant change the staff will experience. Underestimating the change to employees and being unprepared to support them is a critical mistake. A cloud transition is complex; change may not come easily, so include the team from the beginning. To optimize staff, the challenge will be to contrast current staff skills to those needed in the cloud. Start with the basics:
- o   Document current staff size
- o   Inventory the team's skills distribution
- o   Assess their roles, responsibilities and activities
- o   Logistically map staff and their on-premise skills to that needed in the cloud

Develop a Cost Management Strategy to Assess Cloud Provider Pricing Differences

<u>Identifying Costs</u>

Adjusting the IT budgeting model likely has not been a burning problem. Most IT operations have control over their budget. They know where costs are rising. They have a good sense of project costs as well. However, few have administered a cost management system targeted at unpacking how the IT staff spend their time. Meaning, few have reviewed the cost of a particular activity.

Without this information, it is difficult to assess how the cloud pricing will affect recurring expenses. Moving to the cloud will transform the economics of IT. Comparing two types of costing models, CapEx and OpEx, is non-trivial. The effort is time-consuming and difficult. And worse, this will be the financial budgeting environment for a long time.

It is difficult to make data-driven decisions, never mind attempting to divert current legacy budget funds to the cloud transition and the ensuing ongoing OpEx budget expenses. A cost management system is worth using to uncover where costs are and to minimize legacy costs.

Consider Activity Based Costing (ABC) as a cost management methodology. ABC focuses on the staff's activity, which is the most expensive and most valuable resource. Consult the tables in the appendix.

Cloud Pricing

The subscription-based economy is upon us. Accept cloud vendor approaches to subscription prices will vary significantly. Pricing and licensing are different in the cloud. The cloud subscription pricing model (fee to use software) offers predictable recurring fees and is easier to understand and budget (compared to traditional perpetual based licensing). SaaS vendors leading the parade in the cloud all use this model. SaaS offerings are subscription based and are straightforward. Though they vary between vendors, it can be a difficult concept that you don't own any software, and tough to adjust your fiscal budgeting model (from up-front costs to perpetual).

Analyzing pricing details, likely offered with tiers, and participating in the creation of service levels is important. Some cloud pricing models include additional fees for specialized services. Some pricing models also include metering options and are closely coupled to configurations and usage.

CHAPTER 3
Understanding The Cloud Giants' Products and Services

Chapter Outline

- Reviewing the plan this book suggests

- Chapter purpose: Review the cloud giants' products and services

- Categorizing Cloud giants' products and services

  - Cloud Infrastructure, management tools and utilities

  - Data Management and Analytics

  - Application Services

- Cloud giants: The environment they have created and live in

  - The cloud is constantly changing

  - Co-mingling

  - Among the cloud giants, you can't go wrong

- ○ Technology Stalwarts sell their products to reside on multiple cloud giant platforms
- ○ Software licensing options are plentiful
- ○ Standards are great, there is one for everyone!
- ○ Cloud product choices can be found multiple ways
- ○ One stop shopping is here
- ○ Cloud tools are interleaved with all of their product offerings
- ○ Getting out of the plumbing business by entering the cloud. Not so much!
- ○ Blurring lines between the giants and the surrounding cloud vendor marketplace
- ○ Cloud giants' backgrounds
- ○ Born in the cloud giants (AWS, Google, Salesforce, Workday)
- ○ Legacy companies with products and pricing models not originally designed to run in the cloud.
- ○ Summary observations
- Cloud giant product reviews (product sampling)
  - ○ Cloud Infrastructure, management tools and utilities
    - ▪ Provisioning, orchestration and container management tools
    - ▪ Compute Platform
    - ▪ Storage Solutions
    - ▪ Network Content Delivery and Acceleration
    - ▪ Security, Compliance and Identity Management Service
    - ▪ Migration tools
    - ▪ Management tools for all operating management
  - ○ Data Management and Analytics
    - ▪ Databases
    - ▪ Analytic Tools

- o Application Services
  - Development tools
  - Mobile
  - Machine Learning/AI
  - IoT

Reviewing the plan, this book suggests	
Know what the <u>cloud value proposition</u> is and isn't	Chapter 1
Assess your <u>current environment</u>	Chapter 2
Develop a <u>cloud transition strategy</u>	Chapter 2
Learn and compare <u>Cloud giants' products and services</u>	Chapter 3
Learn the <u>cloud marketplace</u>	Chapter 4
Review <u>use case criteria</u>	Chapter 5
Review <u>cost management tables</u>	Appendix

Chapter Purpose: Review the Cloud Giants' Products and Services

The purpose of this chapter is to provide a clear understanding of the cloud giants' product categories. As you read the following cloud product overview, think in terms of the cloud-related actors:

- Cloud giants (AWS, Microsoft, Google, IBM)

- Cloud marketplace (hundreds of the giants' partners)

- IT stalwart vendors with products that run on top of the giants' platforms

- Enterprise customers

This chapter highlights and contrasts the key products and characteristics of four cloud giants: AWS, Microsoft, Google, and IBM. They are wonderful, full-service cloud infrastructure and business solution companies. This chapter, along with Chapter 4 provides Salesforce and Workday product information. They are two of the very best, born-in-the-cloud providers.

The reader may feel there are other cloud giants; however, contrasting these six companies will provide a good overview of the cloud's primary products and services. As you review the giants' products, notice how their products are very similar. Frankly, my research has found none are significantly better than the others.

Though their products have become very similar, their origins couldn't be more different. Consequently, to better understand their fundamental differences, along with reviewing their core offerings, this chapter also reviews the cloud giants' origins, strategy and vision. Reviewing their products and services will help you determine which cloud company(s) may provide the best cloud solutions for your particular needs.

This chapter does not include every product the cloud giants offer; instead, just a sampling. The sampling provides a good sense of the products and how they compare with each other and with your current environment.

Chapter 4 builds upon this chapter and reviews the balance of the cloud marketplace. Chapter 4 also reviews the cloud giants' partnership structures and requirements imposed upon those participating vendors.

Categorizing Cloud Giant Products and Services

Cloud Infrastructure, Management Tools and Utilities

- Provisioning, orchestration and container management tools
- Computing
- Storage
- Network Infrastructure, content delivery, acceleration
- Security and Identity Management
- Migration tools
- Management tools

Data Management and Analytics

- Databases
- Analytic tools

Application Services

- Development platform and tools
- Mobile
- Machine Learning/AI
- IoT

Cloud Giants: The Environment They Have Created and Live In

Before we start with the review of the cloud giant offerings, below are a few thoughts related to the business environment the cloud has created.

The Cloud Is Constantly Changing

The cloud's competitive landscape is anything but clear and undergoing significant change. The old phrase 'the only constant is change' applies when it comes to how the cloud is continuously evolving. Cloud marketplace vendors can experience a service closure, fiscal resource constraints or product innovations that result in changes to customer demand. For example, several large legacy technology companies have decided not to compete with AWS, Microsoft, Google, and IBM in the cloud infrastructure business (i.e., HP, Dell, and VMware), and have discontinued or sold off their core cloud product infrastructure and successfully positioned themselves with different services in the cloud. At the same time, the cloud vendor marketplace has doubled in size during the last few years, generally opting to augment AWS, Microsoft, Google, and IBM cloud infrastructure products.

Co-Mingling

The cloud giants have designed their cloud infrastructures to accommodate each other's products, either through the use of open standards or contractually. For example, Microsoft SQL Server, Active Directory, Exchange Server, Dynamics CRM Dynamics ERP, and SharePoint run on AWS's cloud platform. Cloud giants also have products that are designed to work in a multi-cloud world. The cloud giants' literature frequently highlights interoperability with other cloud products.

Among the Cloud Giants, You Can't Go Wrong

When it comes time to choose a cloud provider for basic compute, storage and network services, all four of the cloud giants highlighted can easily meet the need. All have well-established and viable business models.

Technology Stalwarts Sell Their Products to Reside on Multiple Cloud Giant Platforms

Many well-known Information Technology stalwarts have adjusted their legacy products to host and run on cloud giant platforms. For example, SAP and Adobe run on AWS; Oracle runs on Microsoft; Windows Servers on AWS. Many legacy software applications also run on multiple cloud infrastructures.

Software Licensing Options are Plentiful

Good news: you have options.

Software licensing can include either 'bring your current license' (BYOL) with you to the multi-tenant cloud or purchase the usage rights directly from the cloud provider. For example, the Microsoft software assurance license program (mobility clause) allows for software portability.

For customer license agreements that require complete control one can still move them to the cloud, installing them on dedicated servers (referred to as bare metal).

You can also secure licenses that are integrated with a cloud platform (i.e., Windows Server when spinning up AWS EC2 compute instances, or SQL license when choosing AWS RDS database offerings). Or, when subscribing to a SaaS offering, simply choose the necessary software licenses.

Standards are Great; There Is One for Everyone!

Standards are becoming commonplace with the use of open-source software platforms (i.e., OpenStack, Kubernetes, Docker) for the cloud in areas of computing, networking, and storage. Leading the standards initiative have been well-known companies such as Apache, Redhat, and Rackspace.

Cloud Product Choices Can Be Found Multiple Ways

A review of cloud products will reflect the ability to procure products from one of several product categories. For example,

- Load balancing and VPC functions can be procured and designed into the architecture when building out the compute platform or the network infrastructure.

- Database migration services could either be part of the database selection category or when designing server choices.

- Storage transfer products could be part of a migration strategy or storage strategy.

- The cloud giants also use the terms Artificial Intelligence and Machine Learning interchangeably.

One Stop Shopping Is Here

Cloud giants offer a services-centric model to deliver the infrastructure building blocks including computing, storage, network and database choices, along with a set of disparate tools to support deployments.

All of the cloud giants have tried to simplify their product adoption. For example, product names with multi-functional capabilities include:

- Migration Hubs
- SDKs
- Service Catalog
- Health Dashboard
- Management Console
- Key Management Service
- Mobile Hub
- Cost and Usage Reports

Though the ease of implementation and the capability to quickly secure additional compute and storage has been the cornerstone of all of the cloud giants' value propositions, many practitioners have come to realize it is actually **too** easy to consume resources, and unless costs are watched closely, the model can cost much more than expected.

Cloud Tools are Interleaved with all of Their Product Offerings

Available cloud management tools are numerous and rich in value. They are spread throughout each cloud giant product category. For example, all of the cloud platforms help, regardless of the migration purpose: servers, workloads, databases or the actual data. If you take a closer look at the cloud services, you will find as a common denominator many of the product categories are all about managing data strategies (i.e., storing, moving, or analyzing).

Getting Out of the Plumbing Business by Entering the Cloud. Not So Much!

For anyone that thinks they are getting out of the plumbing business when moving to the IaaS or PaaS cloud environments, not so fast! So, you thought not owning the infrastructure would reduce staff necessary to administer it?

Tasks will remain, such as managing backups, server configuration, performance monitoring, security report review, user account management.

Skills will remain that require system administrators, network engineers, and information security professionals. And those skills are only those needed to manage the basic infrastructure.

Not only are you not getting out of the plumbing business, but your team will need to learn an entire new compute platform architecture. The staff will, of course, also concurrently continue to manage the premise data center until it is decommissioned.

Blurring Lines Between the Giants and the Surrounding Cloud Vendor Marketplace

As time moves forward, the larger cloud marketplace products and service distinctions will become less clear. Many marketplace vendors will continue to provide a service interface with a cloud giant. Vendor reseller offerings can offload the giants' needs to communicate directly with the customer. Also, many marketplace vendors will continue to build competing products with the cloud giants. The cloud marketplace will expand its products to those that simply run on and leverage the cloud giants.

Cloud Giant Backgrounds

Though it is helpful to understand the origins of each cloud giant, because their cloud product lines have grown to be very similar, I have chosen not to spend much time discussing how they came to exist as one of the cloud giants. As mentioned, all four giants provide similar products that are stable, flexible and earn a profit. AWS, for example, reported $23B last year and Microsoft reported $8B in cloud products and services. The cloud giants are continuously leapfrogging each other regarding performance, capability, and price. With large financial reserves, they innovate similarly. All four giants also have very similar availability or uptime service level agreements. Each of the four giants reviewed index their IaaS product line into compute, storage, content delivery, database, and networking. Further, I have not contrasted them along the usual layers (i.e., SaaS, PaaS, IaaS) other than to mention:

- AWS entered the cloud with core infrastructure products and does offer Windows instances.

- AWS uses Reserved instances and Microsoft Azure uses Commitment plans (pricing model when you have a clear understanding of expected usage and reserved capacity). Retrieving the data also has a cost associated with it, not just the compute usage. This pricing choice does require upfront fees and begins to create unused capacity-the very reason (limit unused capacity) you considered cloud-based compute & storage rather than purchasing the gear in the private data centers. Though, the longer the commitment, the lower the costs.

- All cloud giants offer cost calculators to help compare prices of various compute platform sizes, pricing models, related expense elements and costs based upon estimated usage.

- Microsoft entered the cloud marketplace leveraging its existing business software applications. Companies that currently use Microsoft software will have the added value as it will be less disruptive to internal users and customers (not changing software applications). At the same time, most of the Microsoft products will run on the AWS platform as well. Bottom line: often you can continue to use the existing software applications if you chose to.

- Google entered the cloud from a consumer market perspective but has now entered the enterprise space.

Born-in-the-Cloud Giants (AWS, Google, Salesforce, Workforce)

Born-in-the-cloud giants such as AWS, Google, Salesforce, and Workday have the advantage of not needing to protect and drag along existing software that was designed to live in customer data centers.

AWS

Amazon's roots are as an online bookstore from the mid-1990s. Led by Jeff Bezos, the start-up company expanded its offerings to include all sorts of goods and services.

In an effort to meet the online bookstore technology needs, in 2004, Amazon Web Services (AWS) was developed primarily to serve its parent company but quickly expanded to provide computing and storage services for companies on a fee for service basis. AWS became the leader in the IaaS space providing AWS elastic compute capability (EC2) and storage services (S3). Attributes such as pay as you, ability to quickly spin up and down compute capacity as needs require, set the bar for the industry. The model does not include customer ownership of the technology asset (hardware, software), but instead, leases a time-shared platform (referred to as public, multi-tenant).

AWS started with baseline cloud infrastructure products and quickly became the thought leader with a large head start over the others. AWS now provides offerings for all deployment models including Public Cloud, Private Cloud, and Hybrid Cloud.

AWS runs online hosting for software applications offering a range of services including compute cloud, storage, database, and so on.

With a five-year head start, AWS has had the lead with the baseline infrastructure (IaaS) space—but not anymore. The gap is so small today between the giants, that the cloud giants' decisions should not be made at the baseline level (compute, storage, network). AWS has created the largest partner network of all its competitors, as reflected in Chapter 4.

AWS started in the IaaS space, and frequently, new capabilities are announced (maybe too many) and it has stayed mostly true to the IaaS space. However, it is clear they plan to expand their existing database and analytics products, which will move them clearly into the SaaS or PaaS space. For example, the AWS platform offers Elastic Beanstalk, which is an application management platform. They are betting on the fact that business will analyze unstructured data in the cloud. Safe bet!

AWS has entered the artificial intelligence space with voice-activated Alexa. The new AI offering is growing new features weekly.

Google

Google is another born-in-the-cloud company. Its beginnings started at Stanford, running on their servers. Andy Bechtolsheim, one of the co-founders, bought the prospects of the Google search engine in 1998. Larry Page and Sergey Brin designed the search engine called BackRub.

Google's cloud roots started in the consumer business, not the enterprise business/commerce sector. They hired VMware founder Diane Green to head their cloud business. The Google Cloud Platform enables developers to build, test and deploy applications on Google's infrastructure. Google Cloud has computing, storage, and web application services for mobile and backend solutions and competes well with all other cloud giants. The Google Cloud Platform is built on the same infrastructure as Google's search, applications and docs run on. Strive for simplicity is one of their slogans and their platform successfully reflects this design principle.

Salesforce and Workday

I have chosen to also highlight two different cloud giants—Salesforce and Workday—neither of which provide baseline cloud infrastructure services, unless purchasing their product as a SaaS offering. I have chosen to include them as they represent two born-in-the-cloud platforms that are second to none in their respective SaaS offerings.

Salesforce

Where to start when explaining Salesforce is a challenge. Its comprehensive set of products can deliver an immediate ROI and is a good reason to consider Salesforce at the start of a cloud transition. Regardless of how key stakeholders are prioritized (investors, customers or employees), the Salesforce platform of products helps with all three. If you buy into customer interaction as key, then the Salesforce customer relationship management (CRM) software will quickly increase the customer satisfaction ROI.

CRM software originally leveraged strategies and technologies to improve customer interactions through traditional sales and support functions to define and document all customer touchpoint. Arming a sales force with customer information helps improve their sales effectiveness (i.e., account history, contacts, challenges) and ultimately improves customer satisfaction.

Today, CRM software is used for many other types of business functions, from marketing to field service support and everything in between. And Salesforce is the industry leader.

Salesforce is another born-in-the-cloud company and clearly is the darling of the cloud. Salesforce was founded by former Oracle executives Marc Benioff, Parker Harris, Dave Moellenhoff and Frank Domingues. Not unlike Apple, it has built an environment and loyalty among its customer base and partner program that has a fever, cult-like existence. Salesforce does not directly compete in the cloud compute and storage business.

Though their CRM is a world class, best of breed software, Salesforce's value proposition is multifaceted and grown to also include a best of breed development platform (force.com) and a best of breed marketplace (AppExchange). Regarding the environment Salesforce has created, it's hard to tell which of their three platforms add more value, as they are of high value to all of the business world.

Simplified, Salesforce's CRM is built on a native cloud platform (force.com). The Salesforce products cover the entire customer relationship gig, from sales (managing customer interactions), service (i.e., call centers), marketing, collaboration, development integration to Analytics. Salesforce IoT offering is not a device management system but sits on top of those platforms to ingest and make sense of the data.

While there are plenty of CRM platforms (i.e., Microsoft Dynamics, Oracle Siebel, SAP Hybris, IBM Commerce, SAP CRM), Salesforce has the momentum and is the only platform built in the cloud from the outset. Also, though Oracle, SAP, Microsoft, and Adobe all have proven CRM's, none can compete with Salesforce's AppExchange.

With a CRM designed to enhance your understanding of the customer, you would expect Salesforce to also know their customer. And they do. Regardless of which industry; retail, manufacturing, consumer goods, communications, media, government, transportation, automotive, higher education, financial services or health care. Salesforce has a mature set of industry-tailored products.

All of their products are meant to build a deeper customer understanding along with improving the customer experience. Salesforce products help you gain customer sentiment and personalize the customer experience. The goal is to draw a relationship between data collected and your customers. Other important goals include collaboration between sales, service, and marketing.

As business strives to improve and automate tasks along with gaining better analytic insights by developing a more cohesive view of customer data, Salesforce does not disappoint with a feature-rich environment, second to none.

Salesforce Products and Environment Attributes

The Salesforce platform is a market leader with capabilities such as:

- Data management platform
- Social publishing and listening tools
- Data targeting and segmentation
- Measurement tools such as marketing analytics
- Email campaign management
- Campaign analytics
- Internal collaboration tools (e.g., messaging apps, internal social networks)
- Mobile campaign management
- Marketing automation

Note: More information regarding Salesforce AppExchange can be found in Chapter 4.

Workday

Not unlike Salesforce, Workday is another born in the cloud platform. Workday's product provides a SaaS application, focused on large scale ERP (Enterprise Management Processes) systems. It, too, is best of breed both in its service delivery and software functionality. When moving the most important functions of the company operation to the cloud, you simply can't do better. Though there are plenty of ERP choices available, none deliver more value than Workday. Founded in 2005 by PeopleSoft veterans Dave Duffield and Aneel Bhusri, the Workday software has been designed for the world's largest organizations.

An ERP is an integrated suite of software applications that provide common processes and data consistency for human resources, financial management, reporting, analytics, professional services automation, payroll and much more.

Workday's Platform Attributes Include

Service Delivery

- Runs on and uses an open source database

- Updates are continuous, automatic without disruption and ensures the customer is always running on the latest version

- Integration connectors, such as for use with 3rd party payroll systems, exist and are continuously developed by customers, partners, and Workday.

- Not unlike all other public companies, Workday undergos audits for security, privacy controls, and compliance.

- An environment that facilitates feedback ideas and practices between customers and to/from the Workday community.

- Highly qualified implementation partner program exists (more on Workday partner program in Chapter 4).

Functional

- The Workday SaaS application has an employee self-service portal with mobile access for items such as requests for time off, travel reimbursement, and change in benefits.

- Payroll and HR (Human Relations) are fully integrated with one system of record.

- Some industry-specific modules exist. For example, higher education requires product areas such as academic foundation, student recruiting, admissions, curriculum management, student records, academic advising, financial Aid, student financials.

- Have designed and provided machine learning tools to help run the business analytics & big data operations.

Legacy Companies with Products and Pricing Models Not Originally Designed to Run in the Cloud (Microsoft and IBM)

Legacy companies are those with business models based upon premise-based technology solutions, products, and services that were not originally designed to run in the cloud. For example, Microsoft has products such as Dynamics, Office 365, Enterprise Mobility Suite, Windows, SharePoint, and so forth, were not originally designed to run in the cloud.

Legacy companies, such as Microsoft and IBM have the challenge to ensure existing customers who have chosen to move operations to the cloud, don't feel the need to also change their software applications. This places an additional burden on legacy companies to protect their existing products. As a sidebar, such protection requirements often impedes new product development.

Microsoft first tried to protect its premise-based legacy products by dismissing the cloud. They subsequently changed their strategy in a big way, applying enormous resources to build a cloud platform. And they succeeded with a world-class cloud platform, equaling anyone in the playing field. When it comes to delivering new cloud services, Microsoft has delivered a platform that competes with AWS and all the other cloud giants.

Unlike many legacy companies that have had a difficult time transitioning their products from a premise-based delivery model to the cloud, Microsoft has excelled. It helps to have vast fiscal and staff resources, and they have clearly applied them to the cloud.

IBM and Microsoft have taken what has been a liability for most legacy companies and redesigned their products to run in the cloud. Both companies have significant market penetration, independent of the cloud.

Microsoft has turned premise-based legacy software into an advantage, helping its existing customers transition to its cloud platform, Azure. It has done so in a way that has leveraged its highly valued existing premise-based products to strengthen its cloud value proposition.

Because Microsoft products such as Dynamics CRM, Exchange Server, SharePoint, and many others are so well liked and used, Microsoft has an advantage as it can certify these applications on its cloud storage. For example, Microsoft Office 365 is not only one of the best and most used office automation and productivity tool; it lives in the cloud as well. Most users would never know where the application and data reside. Same with MS Dynamics.

With other risk areas to be concerned with during the transition, sticking with Microsoft reduces user disruption and mitigates risk by sticking with the same software. Though, as mentioned, Microsoft tools highlighted above can also run as an instance on other cloud platforms such as AWS.

Prior to building their cloud infrastructure, IBM and Microsoft had built a large and effective partner network. This partner structure also helped them to pivot to becoming strong full-service cloud platforms.

In fact, I suggest that due to the notion that their business penetration and corporate product/services organization is so mature (not to mention top-notch software applications), that they have the advantage in the long term.

As two legacy companies, Microsoft and IBM have met the challenge to transition to the cloud. Microsoft and IBM needed to turn legacy software into an asset, in the cloud, and they did. IBM and Microsoft have done a good job helping to protect their customer's past investments in their products.

Also, Microsoft and IBM not only compete with AWS in the cloud infrastructure space, but they also compete with Salesforce and Workday in the business software area as well.

Microsoft and IBM have additional strengths in Artificial Intelligence and Machine Learning, after decades of developing these key areas. They have truly taken these legacy product lines (built for the premise) which could have acted as a ball and chain and instead leveraged their staff's intellectual capital to reposition these products into the cloud.

This is likely to do with:

- The products are highly functional

- The products are tailored to all market sectors

- Strong world sales and support structures meeting customer needs

- The cost and difficulty for the customers to move to different business software are non-trivial

- Both Microsoft and IBM have exhaustive intellectual and financial capital. It helps to have deep pockets, top-notch staff and deep penetration of well-liked products!

So, even though AWS has been the cloud infrastructure thought leader, if one-stop shopping is important for you (i.e., cloud infrastructure and business software), and possibly you have existing Microsoft or IBM business solutions in place currently, considering Microsoft or IBM in the cloud is a very good idea.

Summary Observations

- All cloud giants have solutions for ingesting, processing, storing, delivering and analyzing video and media content.

- The cloud giants and their surrounding marketplace have blended their storage solutions.

- Microsoft, IBM, and Google have the edge with database services.

- IBM has the best analytic tools and related services but all cloud giants have similar robust tools, and the gap is slim.

- Machine Learning seems to be best served by IBM, Microsoft, and Google.

- VMware has found a couple of cloud dance partners, VMware running on both IBM and AWS cloud platforms.

- All cloud giants have tools that are well thought out and offer capability you may not currently have.

Cloud Giant Product Reviews (AWS, Microsoft, Google, IBM)

The following product listings are not meant to be a complete in depth review of all products, instead it is designed to reflect the cloud giants' product categories, which, as you will notice are thorough and useful. You will note the products are much more similar than different.

Cloud Infrastructure, Management Tools and Utilities

- Provisioning, orchestration and container management tools

- Compute platform

- Storage solutions

- Content delivery network and acceleration tools

- Security, compliance and identity management service

- Migration tools

- Management tools

Product Review: Provisioning, Orchestration and Container Management Tools

(selected products only, not all vendor products are shown)

- **Docker platform to deploy and manage containers such as:**
  AWS Elastic Container Service or Azure Container Instances or Google Container Engine or IBM Containers on Bluemix

- **Kubernetes tools to orchestrate and run containerized applications such as:**
  AWS Elastic Container Service for Kubernetes or Azure Kubernetes Service or Google Kubernetes Engine or IBM Kubernetes Service

- **Registry to store container images as a docker repository such as:**
  AWS Elastic Container Registry or Azure Container Registry or IBM Container Registry

- **Serverless architecture platform and toolsets such as:**
  AWS Serverless Application Repository or IBM OpenWhisk

- **Batch job scheduling capability such as:**
  AWS Batch or Azure Batch Cloud

Service Class Attributes

- Automation capability at its finest
- Provisioning
- Configuration
- Standards-based
- Kubernetes managing Docker containers

All four cloud giants offer self-service and automated provisioning capabilities. Orchestration techniques have been changing, and with the use of new provisioning and configuration tools, you can now standardize your environment to more quickly automate and deploy applications. Whereas virtualization allows an individual application to have a dedicated operating system, containers share the operating system kernel with other containers.

Orchestration is the process of arranging automated and structured processes. Configuration management automates and provisions server configurations.

The cloud giants have embraced the new stack, and each has container management systems and registries to manage the compute platform from creation to deployment to production. The use of these tools is a method of packaging configurations that enable quicker services and improve productivity by deploying a consistent environment.

Kubernetes is a leading open source container orchestration system that assists regardless if you are in a premise-based data center, in a native cloud or a hybrid environment.

The environment also uses Docker containers that enable the virtualization layer to run as an application with the operating system. Think of Docker as an operating system for containers. Docker works by providing a standard way to run your code.

Product Review: Compute Platform

(selected products only, not all products are shown)

- **Dynamically auto-scaled virtual machines such as:**
  AWS EC2 or Azure Virtual Machines or Google Compute Engine or IBM Cloud Virtual Servers

- **Dedicated servers such as:**
  AWS SAM or IBM Bare Metal

Service Class Attributes

- Virtual Machines
- Auto-scaling
- Multiple engine sizes
- Several pricing models
- State of the art tools

The cloud IaaS environment starts with compute capabilities, and none of the cloud giants disappoint. What's not to like; high availability, dynamic scalability, elasticity and tools to automate the platform administration. The compute instances are hosted in multiple locations worldwide (in AWS's case, referred to by regions and zones).

The cloud giants' compute service class tools closely align with each other. Regardless if you are migrating existing workloads to the cloud or building native cloud mobile applications, all of the cloud giants have the compute capability to meet the need. You can even pick the compute processor-AMD or Intel with AWS and Microsoft.

AWS has several instance types from a small Micro tier, nano, general purpose to extra large. Also available are both memory and storage optimized instances, and again, many size choices exist.

All are virtual computing platforms and provide Windows or Linux operating systems along with several pricing models from which to choose.

Virtualization remains heavily used throughout the industry, in addition to the newer orchestration tools mentioned in the provisioning category. With VMware as the most prevalent server virtualization software on the premise, developing a consistent VMware world in both the cloud and on the premise has been a goal of many. To assist its customers with their workload movement to the cloud, AWS and IBM have agreed to be VMware's partners in the cloud (AWS VMware Cloud & IBM VMware Cloud Solutions).

Smart thinking by all three companies (AWS, VMware, and IBM) as VMware owns the lion's share of the premise server virtualization marketplace. VMware products running on both AWS and IBM ease transition efforts by having a consistent environment at both ends.

IBM highlights their private server capability more so than the other cloud giants (although AWS references dedicated servers are also available). I believe this may be to support their long-standing premise-based customers that have previously purchased large scale IBM business software systems (i.e., ERP systems). Some of IBM's customers have bought into the cloud but prefer their own dedicated servers in the cloud. These customers may feel a virtual compute platform, shared with other users, is not secure enough or may be subject to performance issues it can't control in a shared environment.

IBM also offers a bare metal platform running an SAP certified infrastructure. Hence, with their Bare Metal Servers and SAP Certified Infrastructure, IBM has provided their existing customers good reasons to remain an IBM customer, when moving to the cloud. Reducing the risk of losing customers is great thinking, turning a legacy environment into a positive cloud strategy.

IBM has purchased Red Hat and in so doing has made a significant investment in open systems. Even before IBM acquired Red Hat though, the Linux operating system had secured its future in modern computing, as it runs nearly everywhere. The Linux open-source software is a natural fit for needed cloud interoperability and integration. The Linux software is offered at no charge, and its source code is also available.

Product Review: Storage Solutions

(selected products only, not all products are shown)

- **Object based electronic storage such as:**
  AWS Simple Storage service (S3) or Azure Blob Storage or Google Cloud Storage or IBM Object Storage

- **Block based electronic storage such as:**
  AWS Elastic Block Store (EBS) or Azure Disk Storage or Google Persistent Disk or IBM Block Storage

- **NFS file based electronic storage such as:**
  AWS Elastic File System (EFS) or Azure File Storage or IBM File Storage

- **Archive storage for infrequently accessed data (high latency) storage such as:**
  AWS Glacier or Azure Archive Storage

- **Data transfer appliance and tools such as:**
  AWS Snow or Azure Data Box

Service Class Attributes

- Object, block, archiving electronic storage

- Cross-platform file system

- High availability guarantees

- Automatic replication

- Global edge cashing

- Encryption at rest and in transit (using SMB 3.0 and HTTPS)

- Gateway appliances (work with premise-based SAN and NAS environments)

- Low and high latency retrieval speeds

- High throughput for I/O intensive applications

- Data management tools to create, store, retrieve and manipulate data

This service class offers electronic storage, integration appliances, and acceleration tools to facilitate data transfer to the cloud. When considering cloud storage, the task is to review availability, performance, capacity, monitoring tools, access, geo-redundancy and price.

The cloud giants have consistent attributes along, and between their cloud storage products, as such, it is a straightforward comparison. Consistency also exists with their price points and retrieval speeds.

Several selections exist, from object storage to block storage, file storage to archiving storage. The most common form of storage is object storage, accessible using HTTP.

It may be the case the cloud giants have designed a more reliable data storage architecture than many premise-based systems. They also offer hybrid storage appliances connecting on-premise and cloud storage.

All cloud giants have several techniques to help migrate data into their cloud storage products.

The cloud giants all have global infrastructures with caching capability located around the world to reduce latency for frequently retrieved data.

Product Review: Content Delivery Network and Acceleration

(selected products only, not all products are shown)

- **Content delivery network such as:**
  AWS CloudFront or Azure Content Delivery Network or Google CDN or IBM Content Delivery Network

- **Edge devices for local caching such as:**
  AWS Lambda@Edge or AWS Snowball Edge or Google Cloud Interconnect

- **Load balancing tool to distribute incoming traffic across multiple compute instances such as:**
  All have load balancing capability by the same name-load balance

- **VPN gateway services such as:**
  AWS VPC or Azure VPN Gateway or Google Cloud VPN

- **Dedicated private network connections between premise and cloud instances such as:**
  AWS Direct Connect

- **Domain name service such as:**
  AWS Route 53 or Azure DNS or IBM Domain Name Service

- **Network security tools such as:**
  All have tools such as DDoS protection, firewalls, and security groups

- **Optimization and acceleration tools such as:**
  All have optimization and acceleration tools

Service Class Attributes

- Edge caches
- Private and public network connections
- DNS
- Load Balancing
- Security (DDoS denial, firewalls, VPN gateways)

Transitions to the cloud usually involve lengthy timelines; therefore, solid connectivity between the cloud and the premise-based data center is important. Also, as software applications and workloads go live in the cloud, robust global public and private networks with data acceleration techniques such as edge caching devices in order to optimize delivery will be needed.

All cloud giants have installed robust network infrastructures that provide secure state of the art, high-performance throughput, brought about from improved efficiencies, redundancies, multiple carriers, route diversity, and high availability standards. Adequate capacity has been built into the cloud network infrastructure as well. All cloud giants have numerous geographically distributed data centers and regional distribution points that cache data, accelerating content delivery and reducing latency.

Tools are available, such as routers, firewalls, and VPN tunnels to help protect and manage public-facing web content and applications. The tools build private and protected networks, control subnets, connected or isolated.

Common load balancing tools are also available to distribute traffic loads. The tools route traffic based on application or network information (i.e., traffic across multiple EC2 instances). Key attributes include high availability and automation that are integrated with security groups.

As a side note, IBM has partnered with best of breed solutions such as Citrix (NetScaler) or Vyatta gateway Appliances to assist with provisioning multiple environments.

Product Review: Security, Compliance, and Identity Management Service

(selected products only, not all products are shown)

- **Identity and access management system to protect against threats across applications, data, devices, and infrastructure such as:**
  AWS Identity and Access Management or Azure Identity or Google IAM

- **Multi-factor authentication Access control system tools such as:**
  Azure Multi-Factor Authentication or IBM Symantec Two-Factor Authentication

- **Directory service (Microsoft Active Directory) tools such as:**
  AWS Directory Service or Azure Active Directory

- **Secure socket certificate provisioning tools such as:**
  AWS Certificate Manager or IBM SSL Certificates

- **Storage and management tool to manage encryption keys such as:**
  AWS Cloud HSM or Azure Key Vault or Google Cloud Key Management Service or IBM Hardware Security Module

- **Encryption keys tools such as:**
  AWS Key Management services or Google Security Key Enforcement

- **Portal to provide comprehensive data risk platform and unified security access tools such as:**
  AWS Artifact or Azure Security Center or Google Cloud Security Command Center or IBM Cloud Identity

- **Threat Protection tools such as:**
  AWS Guard Duty or Azure Advanced Threat Protection

- **Single sign-on Service and access control tools such as:**
  AWS Single sign-on or AWS Cognito or Google Firebase Authentication

- **Firewall tools such as:**
  AWS Firewall Manager or AWS WAF or IBM Hardware Firewall or IBM Dedicated Hardware Firewall or IBM High Availability Firewall or IBM Fortigate Security Appliance

- **Denial of service tools such as:**
  AWS Shield or Azure DDoS Protection

- **Compliance services and audit documents access tools such as:**
  AWS Artifact or AWS Inspector

Service Class Attributes

- Identity Management
- Single sign-on (authentication and authorization)
- Compliance and Risk Management tools and support
- Encryption in transit and at rest
- Firewall protection
- Threat detection
- DDoS protection
- Monitoring tools
- Phishing
- Ransomware, viruses, worms, trojans

Security is a Team Sport!

Consider thinking of shared cloud security responsibilities with three participants:

- Customer
- Cloud Giant
- Cloud Marketplace Vendor

An important task when entering the cloud is to rate the security compliance level of each cloud service.

The cloud giants have created a shared responsibility model regarding the management of the stack layers, including security. Service level agreements (SLA) assist in ensuring expectations are met.

The transition to the cloud has increased security risks for organizations. The cloud giants are aware and have put together a layered defense approach with resilient security platforms to protect data theft. Their security products also help protect against service disruption attacks. Risk compliance products and services also exist.

They assist with security assessments, provide transparent compliance documents and work to obtain certifications. They address security incidents that monitor, detect and respond to threats. They also have a keen awareness of the institutional bodies and compliance agencies that govern their actions.

The cloud giants have put in place an information technology security practice that is equal or better than most premise-based security frameworks. Security is built-in in every way to protect it all; infrastructure, applications, data and identity. A security mindset is woven into their entire company culture, not just information technology-related decisions. Their entire corporate culture has security at the forefront of everything it does. The cloud giants provide documents that cover areas such as:

- Their practices to manage and protect data risks.
- Directives, guidelines and country standards documents

- Single sign on SAML 2.0 and OpenID that work with large scale ERP and CRM vendors

- Undergo verifications of privacy and their compliance controls.

They know and follow compliance laws, standards and regulations such as:

- PCI, HIPAA,COBRA,FERPA,

- NIST 800-53 Security and privacy requirements for US federal information systems

- Sarbanes-Oxley Act (SOX) (improving the accuracy and reliability of corporate disclosures

- ISO 27001,27017,27018

- Service Organization Control (SOC) reports.

Product Review: Migration Tools

(selected products only, not all products are shown)

- **Migration service for databases, servers, and data or a combination of all three, including data import/export and discovery tools such as:**
  AWS Snowball, AWS Migration Hub or AWS Server, Data, Database Migration Service or Azure Database Migration Service or Azure or Google Cloud Storage Transfer Service or Azure Database Migration Service Google BigQuery Data Service or IBM Lift or IBM Mass Data Migrations or IBM VMware Cloud Solutions or AWS Data Pipeline or AWS Application Discovery Service

- **Data transfer appliance (premise-based) such as:**
  AWS Snow or Azure Data Box or IBM Transfer Appliance

- **VMware workload transfer tool such as:**
  IBM VMware Cloud Solution

Service Class Attributes

- Migrate databases, applications, servers, data
- Integrate
- Accelerate
- Recovery
- Premise-based transfer appliances
- Track migrations from a single pane of glass
- Discover tools for premise-based applications to streamline migration

The cloud giants have been wise again, providing products and services that help migration your data to their cloud infrastructure. The assembled set of tools simplify and accelerate the migration to the cloud. The outcome is the ability to move legacy applications and data to the cloud using their tools and services. If you choose a lift and shift migration model these tools will assist.

Some of the product names are intuitive, as you expect and want. The main services and tools are:

- Appliances (on-premise) to move data to the cloud
- Command line tools to move data
- Tools to move entire databases
- Services to assist

Product Review: Management Tools for All Operations Management

(selected products only, not all products are shown)

All four cloud giants offer nearly the same management tool products, and many are without a unique name. Therefore, the cloud giants' management-related tools are simply listed by function below. The service class attributes list should give you a good understanding and appreciation for the thoughtfulness and completeness of an integrated set of tools.

Service Class Attributes

- Steady state operations management
  - Deploy
  - Automation/provisioning/configuration/update
  - Real-time monitoring for services, containers, applications, and infrastructure
  - Set policies
- Notification service tool to push messages to recipients
- Simplified backup and recovery tool
- Data collection tools
- Diagnostic performance and troubleshooting tools for web applications and other systems
- Automated scripting to configure, deploy and invoke scheduled work more quickly
- Log tools to collect and analyze data and user activities
- Portal, hub or central integrated management console to manage all products
- Error reporting tool
- Resource consumption tool
- Data collection and analyzation tool
- Event management tool for incident correlation

- Recording and compliance tools
- Tools that look across multiple cloud providers
- Billing, cost assessment and management
- Site recovery
- Built-in disaster recovery service
- Trace performance bottlenecks
- Traffic manager-route incoming traffic for high performance and availability

On the premise, many information technology operations use old inefficient management tools. As a result of staff acquiring specialty tools over the years, most current management tool kits are a hodgepodge of outdated tools. Tools that make it more difficult to troubleshoot problems, never mind anticipate issues. And certainly, the existing tools were not designed for or have the capability to work well in the cloud.

It is my hunch the comprehensive set of tools offered by all the giants, along with their integrated nature, compares favorably to many current environments.

I've mentioned the opportunity and importance of re-architecting the existing information infrastructure when moving to the cloud. When adopting cloud management tools, the opportunity to dispose of old, unintegrated tools in favor of state-of-the-art cloud management tools is another strategic win.

The tools enable the creation, storage, retrieval and manipulation of data. This enables the automation, monitoring, provisioning, and ability to maintain control of your entire environment. An environment that keeps applications secure both in the cloud and the private data center.

Google has the usual suspects with a collection of integrated tools under the marketing term referred to as Stackdriver. The Google management tool suite also has the added value of performing in both the Google and AWS clouds.

Data Management and Analytics

- Databases
- Analytic tools

Product Review: Databases

(selected products only, not all products are shown)

- **Relational databases such as:**
  AWS RDS MYSQL, AWS Aurora, IBM DB2, PostgreSQL, SQL Server or Google Cloud SQL-MySQL and PostgreSQL database service or IBM Compose for MySQL-RDBMS database or IBM Compose for PostgreSQL

- **Non-relational databases such as:**
  AWS DynamoDB NoSQL, Google Cloud Datastore or IBM Cloudant, MongoDB Redis, Cassandra, HBase

- **Data warehouses such as:**
  AWS Redshift or Azure SQL data warehouse-elastic warehouse as a service

- **Managed Database Services and Database Migration Services are offered by each of the cloud giants.**

- **In memory data store such as:**
  Google Cloud Memorystore or IBM Database for Redis

Service Class Attributes

- Bring your own database instance
- Host the database on the cloud giants' virtual servers
- Subscribe to a database in the cloud (SaaS)
- Open source databases
- SQL databases

- SQL Servers
- MySQL
- NoSQL
- Data Warehouses

Each of the cloud giants has enterprise class databases and services. Throughout the book, I have maintained the idea that there is merit to seize the moment when moving to the cloud and re-architect the infrastructure (technology, skills, processes). Reviewing the use of your databases is yet another opportunity to re-architect.

Regarding databases, the type of re-architecting I suggest lies with the data itself more so that changing databases. Rather than moving a legacy application to a new cloud database, which can be very time consuming and disruptive, consider where the application is in its life cycle

Even if you wish to change databases, it may not be possible as the legacy application doesn't support a different database or the application is old and not worthy of the effort to switch to a different database. Many of the database services are closely tied to specific use cases, which may mandate the type of database you need. Meaning, let the application drive which database you use, not the cloud. However, if building a new application is the task, the cloud giants have the type of database to support it.

Though AWS started in the compute and storage cloud services business, the list of offered AWS databases confirm the AWS platform is much more than just compute, storage and networking. Also, AWS and the other cloud giants provide the ability to run either Oracle or Microsoft SQL on their respective platforms.

The database tools available to automate and assist are functionally rich, from installing the database to disk provisioning or backup and recovery of databases. The database product offerings are also able to use automated synchronous replication capabilities that are housed in geographically dispersed locations.

All cloud giants provide a choice of several database services. Database migration choices exist, ranging from migrating and maintaining the current premise located database to porting or re-platforming or simply building a new cloud native database. The cloud giants can assist with your chosen approach.

Product Review: Analytic Tools

(selected products only, not all products are shown)

- **Hadoop platform such as:**
  AWS EMR, Azure HDI or Google Cloud Dataproc or IBM Hadoop

- **Streaming Analytic tools such as:**
  AWS Kinesis or Azure Stream Analytics or Azure Apache Storm for HDInsight or Google Cloud Pub/Sub or IBM Streaming Analytics

- **Data Warehouse platform such as:**
  AWS Redshift or Azure SQL Data Warehouse, Google Big Query or IBM DashDB

- **Data Visualization products such as:**
  AWS QuickSight or Azure Power BI Embedded or Google Cloud Datalab or IBM Cognos Dashboard Embedded

- **Predictive Analytic tools such as:**
  Azure R Server for HDInsight or IBM Watson

- **All-purpose tools (i.e., query, data discovery, conversion, mapping, scheduling) such as:**
  AWS Glue or AWS Log Analytics or Azure Data Lake Analytics or Google Cloud Dataprep or IBM Cognos

- **Statistical tools such as:**
  IBM SPSS

Service Class Attributes

- Tools also used in many of the other service classes
- Predictive analytics
- Hadoop distributions
- Warehouses and operational data stores
- Data discovery
- Query tools
- Analyze streaming data in real time
- Data integration tool
- Structured and Unstructured data

Investments in analytics tools, though complex and expensive, helps us learn from what the data can tell us. For example, mining unstructured and structured data can help understand customer preferences and sentiments.

For any decision, you need data. In data-rich markets you can review existing data or go get new data. For years companies wisely took advantage of data availability and have been actively building predictive models that strive to use the vast amount of data they collect to better understand the past and to better anticipate the shape of the future. They have gathered, analyzed and shared data for decades; however, today, more data is arriving than ever before and at a quicker pace.

The challenge is to choose the right cloud products to better predict the future, to ask the right questions and choose the right things to measure.

Needed is to develop a data science team to create a framework that identifies key properties of data and how data sets are related. The framework requires tools to cleanses the data and ensure the data is useful and actionable.

When selecting the correct analytic tools, look for machine learning tools that best check for validity and help identify data attributes. Required are tools that help move from just descriptive to predictive capability. Strive to select tools that provide the best keyword, semantic or contextual search data. Assess tools that define properties and relationships among data. These are the attributes to keep in mind as you review cloud analytical tools.

Using Hadoop distributions in the cloud is also an option. Hadoop is helpful to mine unstructured data and its use helps promote sound decision making as it speeds up business agility. Because mining unstructured data consumes a great deal of space, and the cloud has the capacity to store large sums of data, building a Hadoop environment in the cloud is a cost-effective choice.

In my judgment, of the cloud giants, IBM has superior analytical products and services. IBM has a long-standing ability, long before the cloud, to make sense of data, focus and assist with deciding where to place the investment with business intelligence and predictive analytics.

Introduction to the Third of the Product Review Categories: Application Services

The balance of the cloud service areas listed in this chapter is more closely tied to increasing revenue than reducing expenses. Call it business intelligence, data visualization or big data; we have arrived at one of the most important areas of managing information technology. These tools provide methods and techniques that help measure performance. A close relationship exists between Artificial Intelligence, Machine learning, Analytics and Internet of Things (IoT).

Also, just a quick note to mention that numerous tools sets could be placed in several cloud service class areas, for example:

- IBM's DB2 Event Store is an in-memory database, but it is also a purpose built as an analysis tool.

- Data visualization tools can be found in several service classes, including machine learning, analytics, mobile application development or databases.

- Microsoft Azure Stream analytics is real time processing for IoT and it can be found in the Analytic service class and the IoT category.

- API Gateways and tools are sprinkled in several service classes including development tools, analytics, integration and IoT.

- IBM Watson, Google Analytics Suite of products or Microsoft Revolution R Enterprise or Cloudera/Hortonworks are great products to consider and are useful in a multitude of ways.

Application Services

- Development tools

- Mobile

- Machine Learning/AI

- IoT

Product Review: Development Tools

(selected products only, not all products are shown)

- **Automated code deployment tools such as:**
  AWS CodeDeploy or IBM Workload Scheduler

- **Code development tools such as:**
  AWS CodeBuild or AWS CodeStar or IBM Globalization pipeline

- **Developer toolsets such as:**
  AWS CodePipeline or Google Dev Tool SDK

- **Test environments (reusable templates) such as:**
  Azure DevTest Labs or Reusable templates or Google Firebase test lab

- **API platform such as:**
  Google Apigee API Platform

- **Visualization tools such as:**
  Azure Visual Studio Code or Google tools for Visual Studio or Google Maven app engine plug in

- **Combine cloud services with open source and third-party tools such as:**
  IBM Toolchain

Service Class Attributes

- Tools to build, deploy and manage multi-platforms. For example, AWS offers three delivery methods; Machine image, CloudFormation Stack and SaaS

- Command line tools and interfaces

- Code sharing, monitoring, and tracking tools

- Templates for test labs

- Analyze and debug tool integrations (Eclipse, IntelliJ, Maven), GCP (Eclipse and Maven)

- Source repositories to store, manage and track code

- Log analysis to collect, store and analyze app log data

- Performance and load testing for DevOps

Compare your developer tools to theirs!

Many of the current premise-based application development environments include tools and techniques acquired over many years and do not reflect an architecture of integrated and best of breed tools. In fact, many of the tools are no longer used. Transitioning to the cloud provides a chance to acquire newer more integrated tools. You will likely also attract new IT talent or inspire existing staff as the integrations tools and development methodologies used in the cloud will excite any good developer.

Modern cloud development methodologies can involve a blended set of cloud company products. For example, one could use AWS CodeDeploy, AWS Elastic Beanstalk, and AWS OpsWorks, obviously running on AWS. Or, also using the AWS platform, Microsoft development tools such as Visual Studio, PowerShell, and .NET Developer Center is a possibility. The goal is to complete and deploy code faster and with lower risk.

Product Review: Mobile Application Development Platform

(selected products only, not all products are shown)

- **Software development kits such as:**
  AWS Mobile SDK or Azure Mobile Apps or IBM Mobile Foundation

- **Mobile build and monitor tool such as:**
  AWS Mobile Hub or Azure Xamarin or IBM App Launch

- **API tool kit such as:**
  Azure API Apps or Azure Maps or Google Apigee API

- **Test devices (Android, iOS, web apps)**

Service Class Attributes

- Mobile analytics
- API Gateway
- Mobile applications
- Mobile SDK's
- Notification tools

It's All About Mobile Applications, Right?

There is a close relationship between tools used when developing web applications, API connectors and mobile applications in production. As such, many of the same development tools are used in all three environment methodologies. They all provide user authentication and user profiles, along with push notifications to all devices and APIs.

At their core, they are developer tools used to create, configure, build, test, maintain and monitor usage of all cloud developed applications. Testing tools are also available for use with Android, iOS and web apps.

The APIs assist when accessing backend services and workloads. When processing API calls, a cost is incurred (i.e., when transferring and receiving data). Typically, the use of a mobile SDK (software development kit) supports languages such as Ruby, Java, and PHP. The SDKs usually provide many pre-built APIs.

Product Review: Machine Learning/Artificial Intelligence

(selected products only, not all products are shown)

- **Machine learning models such as:**
  AWS SageMaker or AWS TensorFlow (open source machine intelligence library), AWS Deep Learning AMI, AWS Kinesis, Azure Python packages or IBM Watson Studio or Google Machine Learning Engine or Google Cloud IoT core

- **Search tools (entity, web, video, news) and mining unstructured data such as:**
  Azure Bing Video Search or Google Cloud Natural Language

- **Speech to text conversion such as:**
  Azure Translator Speech or Azure Bing Speech or Google Cloud Speech to Text

- **Text to Speech conversion such as:**
  Google Cloud text to speech or IBM Watson Text to Speech

- **Analyze sentiment from text such as:**
  Azure Text Analytics or IBM Watson Natural Language

- **Machine learning models for image classification such as:**
  Azure ML Package for Computer Vision or Azure Computer Vision or IBM Deeplens (deep learning enabled video camera)

- **Search for news such as:**
  Azure Bing News Search

- **Derive data from videos such as:**
  Google Video Intelligence

- **Streaming tools such as:**
  Azure Stream Analytics

- **Machine learning engine platform such as:**
  Azure Machine Learning service, Google Advanced Solutions Lab

- **Analyze images and video such as:**
  Rekognition

Service Class Attributes

- Visualization tools

- Building and training deep learning Artificial Intelligence models

- Niche Search capabilities

- Translation and conversion tools and services

- Data targeting and segmentation

- Machine Language algorithms

Hurry! Make the cloud giant infrastructure product decisions (i.e., storage, compute, network, security platforms) in order to allow an increased focus on products that will more directly contribute to growing the business. Machine learning and artificial intelligence tools is a service class that will improve business ROI. Developing predictive insights across data and systems are key to better understanding of market opportunities. The tools listed in this section are one of the richest set of products of all the service classes.

The machine learning and artificial intelligence service class provides deep learning tools and many specialty search and translation tools. For example, specialty search and translation tools are available for many data types and sources (i.e., web, visual, video, spell check, news, entity, images, auto-suggest and custom data). These machine learnings tools enable emotion recognition, overcome noise and speech style often found in data & face and speaker recognition and identify metadata. Cloud inference APIs and prediction tools also help identify groups, as determined by their predicted behavior. And the cloud giants also offer these tools via a fully managed service.

When reviewing cloud content management platforms, Salesforce should also be considered; they provide customer segmentation tools that personalize content by delivering sentiment analysis to the right business channel. Salesforce tools along with vendors in the Salesforce AppExchange marketplace are among the best tools available.

Accelerator technology at its finest! All cloud giants use their products to provide a comprehensive IoT solution designed to quicken the development of Artificial Intelligent (AI) workloads. Each cloud giant has developed AI products that work together to run, train and accelerate the end to end environment. These tools are designed to ingest data from almost any device in the world. Further, the tools allow you to process and analyze the data in real time. They use MQTT and HTTP protocols to push out firmware updates. The hardware chip sets are designed for low latency with high performance. They enable the development of AI models and typically run on the cloud edge to improve performance. The products are a combination of open software, AI algorithms, and hardware.

Product Review: Internet of Things

(selected products only, not all products are shown)

- **Ingest and stream real-time device data, configure, connect, register devices such as:**
  AWS Greengrass or IBM IoT Hub or IBM Watson IoT Platform or Azure IoT Hub or Google Edge IoT Core or AWS IoT Core or Azure Insight

- **Run Machine Language models at the edge such as:**
  IBM Edge TPU or Azure IoT Edge

- **Accelerator technology such as:**
  Google Edge TPU

- **IoT security such as:**
  AWS IoT device defender

Service Classes attributes

- Accelerator technology

- Closely related to Machine Learning service class

- Collecting or data capture, analyzing, pushing data to/from devices outside of the cloud

- Core IoT products manage data, integrate, analyze and trigger actions

- Process device events

- Uses edge devices to reduce latency

- Devices, applications, sensors, web sites

All cloud giants have invested in IoT Device management systems to harness big data to gain insight. The IoT products allow devices of all types, via MQTT protocols, to communicate with each other or with existing production applications. Machine learning and artificial intelligence are run on IoT software. APIs are used within the applications to assist the communication. The products extend cloud intelligence and analytics to edge devices to better manage the remote assets. The products stream and transmit data to cloud endpoints. Constant communications between cloud applications and devices enables their management. Examples include interpreting and analyzing data, configuring and registering devices and sensors that enable the ability to automatically act on information received.

CHAPTER 4
Understanding the Cloud Marketplace

Chapter Outline

- How to use the cloud marketplace

- A marketplace with global reach: The real secret sauce

- The cloud marketplace defined

- The cloud marketplace vendor considerations

- Everyone wins! Relationships between giants, the marketplace vendors and the customer

- Cloud vendor partnership requirements (as imposed by cloud giants)

- Tiered structure between the cloud giants and their partners

- Sample listing of cloud marketplace vendor product categories and services

  o Cloud Infrastructure, management tools and utilities

  o Data Management and Analytics

- o Application Services
- o Example 1: Sample functionality of a marketplace vendor product (security)
- o Example 2: Sample of cloud marketplace partnering (VMware & AWS, VMware & IBM)
- Workday marketplace
- Salesforce marketplace

Chapter Purpose: How to Use the Cloud Marketplace

This chapter defines the cloud marketplace, outlines how it is organized, lists numerous service categories and outlines the relationship between the marketplace vendors and the cloud giants. Knowledge of this type will enable successful marketplace vendor choices.

The chapter will show how to leverage the cloud marketplace and contrast the different marketplace partner programs. This insight will also help protect from continuous changes within the vendor marketplace and highlight their competitive differentiation. Just as the cloud giants are expanding and contracting, the cloud marketplace is changing in much the same way.

As reflected throughout this book, due diligence is necessary in several key areas in order to successfully transition to the cloud. Learning the cloud marketplace is one of those areas, as surrounding yourself with good cloud marketplace vendors is critical. Determining which marketplace vendors have developed a sustainable path forward is a critical selection component.

A Marketplace with Global Reach:
The Real Secret Sauce

The value of the marketplace is to gain access to additional technical skills, expertise, and meaningful guidance. The cloud marketplace does not disappoint. Companies that have thrived in the cloud marketplace have tremendously expanded their services, products, and strategies. Though the cloud is very large, the 80/20 rule applies with most cloud services handled by a small number of companies.

The marketplace receives resources from the giants in areas of training, certification programs, and market awareness. In return, the cloud giants receive value from the marketplace as they strive to improve and sell off its core services.

The marketplace vendors provide software solutions and services. The cloud giants have vetted and verified the vendors in their partner programs. As a result, the giants can ensure top quality partners that are successful in their chosen specialty. These vendors can help make decisions in areas such as the infrastructure, cloud operations and assess needed skills and knowledge. For example, they can help ensure workloads are portable across cloud platforms. As you begin to vet the cloud vendors for yourself, obligate time to conduct proof of concepts and fully review their products.

Many of the cloud marketplace products and services are tailored to specific industries and channels of business, while others are usable by nearly all industries.

Reviewing the cloud marketplace will enable the discovery of their magnitude and potential. Assessing the cloud marketplace products and services sets the stage to more fully value their applied use, as outlined in Chapter 5 use case criteria.

The cloud marketplace leverages and creates extensive use of both the cloud giants' products and their own products and services. Most are built upon the giants' cloud platforms.

The cloud marketplace vendors offer services to help build, design, manage and migration services. Consider three service provider categories:

- Bellwether companies that run their business application software on the cloud giants' infrastructures, such as SAP and Oracle run on AWS. Or VMware runs on AWS and IBM.

- Relatively new, native cloud marketplace startup companies, most of which did not exist prior to the cloud.

- Well-established IT companies running their infrastructure products and services on the giants' platforms.

The Cloud Marketplace Defined

Most of the cloud marketplace vendors have aligned with one or more cloud giants. The cloud giants' structured partnering programs are very helpful as it strengthens both the cloud giants and the marketplace vendors quality of service, having previously established clear skill levels, product awareness, and vendor financial strength.

As outlined in chapter three, the cloud giants' offerings are very similar to each other. The cloud marketplace structures are similar to each other as well.

The partnership arrangement between the cloud giants and the marketplace vendors is a traditional one. It is indexed either by service or technology, is a tiered model with cloud marketplace vendors requirements well spelled out.

The vendor marketplace extends the reach and capability of core cloud services, offered by the cloud giants. It also provides for the design and growth of vendor products that run atop the cloud giants' infrastructures.

The giants are, in their most basic form, online stores that enable the purchase and deployment of cloud software and services. It follows then that the surrounding cloud marketplace vendors are also online stores (via structured partnership guidelines with the cloud giants). The cloud marketplace vendors are stores with services and products meant to assist customers better leverage cloud giants' services. The marketplace has useful products and services that extend the value of the giants' products.

Both the cloud giants and the surrounding marketplace vendors are cloud service providers. The Marketplace is large, in a constant state of flux, and this complicates their use. The partner alignment continues.

The marketplace vendors can offer best practices for designing reliable, secure, efficient, and cost-effective systems in the cloud.

Use of marketplace vendors increases the likelihood of business success. The cloud marketplace has a wide variety of business verticals and use cases. The cloud marketplace is cut along industry sectors and solution sets.

The cloud marketplace can:

- Help assess
- Help implement
- Provide services that run on the cloud giants' infrastructures
- Show how to save money
- Broker services
- Mitigate risk
- Assist building a cloud architecture
- Migrate data and applications

You will find most cloud marketplace vendors are outstanding at what they do and they will be willing to help you with your cloud transition. Some are aligned to cloud giants via their partnership programs, and some are not. Companies new and old are partnering in the cloud with new products and services, and it is a very competitive environment.

Cloud Marketplace Vendor Considerations

When interviewing marketplace vendors consider criteria such as:

- Credibility
- Security transparency and capability
- Uptime history and commitments
- Breadth and depth of offerings
- Their product ease of use

Though not yet fully accomplished, all giants and their surrounding marketplaces have created an environment that strives to:

- Automate product selections
- Highlight licensing and pricing options
- Aluminate user agreements
- Simplify billing and usage

Determining which set of cloud marketplace vendors best suit your needs will take some time. Their evaluation will be based upon which cloud system is to be installed and how they may be able to assist. Evaluate vendors today for the environment of tomorrow.

Everyone Wins! Relationships Between Giants, the Marketplace Vendors, and the Customer

- Typical cloud giant offerings provided to their partners consist of items such as:
  - Business, technical and sales resources
  - Access to key development managers
  - Co-branding opportunities (marketing campaigns, webinars, case studies)
  - Training, accreditations, and certifications
- Cloud marketplace vendors assist organizations to deploy web applications running on the giants' cloud platforms.
- The cloud marketplace vendors expand the giants' infrastructures with value-added features and service.
- The customer will gain access to cloud marketplace vendors that understand the cloud giants' products and gain valuable implementation experience.

Partnership Requirements (as Imposed by Cloud Giants)

In order to maintain security, standards, and mitigate risk the cloud giants have imposed partnership program requirements such as:

- Sell publicly available, full-feature, production-ready software (not in Beta)
- Maintain an established customer support operation
- Maintain software products for vulnerabilities
- Maintain a good relationship with the cloud giant for which they are partnered with
- Identify any outsourced functionality
- Abide by best practice security policies and procedures

- Have business continuity plans

Tiered Partnership Structure Between the Cloud Giants and Their Partners

As mentioned, the cloud giants' partner structures are generally indexed into either technology partners or service partners. The technology section has vendors with application software. The service section has vendors with consulting services.

Think in terms of technology partners that provide tools and software infrastructure. The tools category could be further indexed into developer kits, business & productivity software, and infrastructure.

Contrasting the cloud giants' partnership structures, you find they all have structures that are based upon competency partner levels. Nothing unusual here. For example,

Competency Categories		
AWS	**Microsoft**	**Google**
Premier	Silver	Premier
Advanced	Gold	Authorized
Standard		Registered
Registered		

Sample Listing of Cloud Marketplace Vendor Product Categories and Services

Cloud Infrastructure, Management Tools and Utilities

- Compute Platform, including serverless and high-performance computing
- Storage solutions
- Content Delivery Network, including data acceleration tools, software-defined networking, load balancing and caching services
- Security, Compliance and Identity Management Service
- Migration tools, planning, architecting and building (data, servers, database)
- Management tools
- Business continuity (disaster recovery, archiving, backup and restore)
- Monitoring in a hybrid world
- Provisioning and automating the stack
- Cloud pricing tools

Data Management and Analytics

- Databases
- Business Intelligence, warehouses, big data, analytic tools, mining unstructured and structured data
- Master data platform management products

Application Services

- Application development tools, including mobile development platforms, tools, and services
- Machine Learning/AI

- IoT
- Media Services
- Integration (APIs and connectors)
- Automating/streamlining business & workload processes
- E-commerce & Websites
- Email and Messaging and collaboration
- Content Management
- ERP
- CRM
- Gaming

The cloud marketplace structure is tailored to the specific needs of its customers. Below are two examples that highlight both the depth and breadth of vendor products and the type of partnering that occurs in the cloud.

Example 1: Sample Functionality of a Marketplace Vendor Security Product (Security)

Below, take a look at the functionality of a cloud marketplace vendor product, as it relates to data security. It is a very impressive list of valuable products and services.

- Virtual Private Network
- Secure Back-up
- 2-factor authentication
- Firewalls
- Virtual routers
- Encryption
- Scanning
- Email monitoring

- Endpoint

- Intrusion detection

- LDAP & AD support

- Identity management

- Denial of Service

- Filtering incoming data

- Single pane of glass

- Manage passwords

- Compliance

- Database security

I picked a cloud marketplace security provider's suite of products not only as an example of a service offered, but also to reinforce the idea presented earlier that security is taken seriously in the cloud, both by the giants and the vendor marketplace.

Want more proof, take a look at either IBM's or Google's white papers on the topic.

Example 2: Sample of Cloud Marketplace Partnering (VMware & AWS, VMware & IBM)

An example of the value of the cloud marketplace partnering can be found when reviewing VMware and AWS or VMware and IBM.

Simply said, you can run VMware on AWS or IBM cloud infrastructures. The meaningfulness of this partnering rests with the improved ease of blending premise based virtual environments with either the AWS or IBM cloud platforms.

VMware running in the cloud and the private data center more easily creates a hybrid environment for tasks such as replicating capabilities needed for routine backup or business continuity solutions. Another example may be found when busting into the cloud for added capacity.

Workday Marketplace

As mentioned in chapter three, Workday functionality is second to none and is a native cloud company with expertise in financial and human capital management.

Its marketplace partner program is straightforward and rational, focusing on the important items of implementation, integration and large-scale project management.
Partner categories:

- Software partners

- Global payroll partners

- Service partners

- Certified Solutions partners

- Workday connect partners (connect 3rd party payroll systems)

- Preferred integration partners (partners and customers build their own integrations)

Workday's partners are some of the best in the world and are well vetted by Workday. The established Workday marketplace is designed to quickly and easily move 3rd party or legacy systems into the cloud-based Workday software. And, Workday continuously trains and supports these member marketplace companies.

Global partners provide software such as:

- Time and attendance

- Workforce screening

- Secure e-signature

- Document management

- Talent management

- Imaging and OCR

- Enterprise content management

- Process automation
- Health management system

Salesforce Marketplace

If there is a smarter partner program than Salesforce's, I have not seen it. Salesforce refers to its marketplace as the AppExchange. The AppExchange is an ecosystem second to none. It is likely the most meaningful marketplace of all the giants. The Salesforce AppExchange has the traditional service and consulting partners to assist with core Salesforce product implementations. They are much the same as those implementation partners found in Workday, IBM and Microsoft.

However, the Salesforce AppExchange consists of much more, to include pre-built applications, pre-built templates, pre-built integrations, and access to data and tools to build your own applications, including a mobile platform service. The AppExchange is also a collection of applications from many third-party companies that extend the value of the core Salesforce products. These applications in the Salesforce AppExchange are vetted by Salesforce.
It is possible the AppExchange partner program is equal in value to their flagship CRM product. As companies join the Salesforce AppExchange, Salesforce helps them build applications more quickly (AppCloud). In doing so, Salesforce markets the partner product on their AppExchange platform. Salesforce uses a shared revenue model with its partners. The Salesforce cloud program:

- Helps build a sales strategy (i.e. go to market and customers creation)
- Provides resources such as training, certification programs and planning support
- Assists to develop a solid salesforce practice
- Screens applications for security
- To reduce development time, provides access to Salesforce experts and the partner community

CHAPTER 5
Cloud Solutions

Chapter Outline

Use Case Criteria 1: Migrating Data, Applications, and Servers to the Cloud

Use Case Criteria 2: Developing a Cloud Integration Platform

Use Case Criteria 3: Preparing for Cloud Storage

Use Case Criteria 4: Data Management

Use Case Criteria 5: Analytics

Use Case Criteria 6: Content Delivery Services

Use Case Criteria 7: Security, Risk Management and Identity Management Systems

Use Case Criteria 8: Machine Language Modeling

Use Case Criteria 9: Application Development in the Cloud

Use Case Criteria 10: Database Decisions

Chapter Introduction

This chapter provides key criteria necessary to help shape ten potential use cases. All ten use a combination of cloud marketplace products to drive value from the cloud.

The categories highlight Information Technology management areas in need of improvement regardless of the cloud. Though there is a great deal of cloud technology to learn, there is also the need, independent of the cloud, to first assess business goals, simplify processes and clean up data. Therefore, to be successful with any of the use case categories outlined, the following fundamental areas of need exist:

- Focus on business-related objectives, first:
    o Create a prioritized set of required business outcomes
    o Assess business officers' willingness to contribute to cloud transition efforts (i.e. a process of inclusion).
    o Review existing software applications to determine which are cloud candidates, which need improvement before moving to the cloud and which are reaching their end of life.
- Continuous management of Information Technology resources:
    o Put in motion a staff skills transformation plan
    o Conduct an assessment of current provisioning methods (internal to IT operations), with an eye toward self-service.
    o An assessment of the current infrastructure age and capacity
    o Ability to accelerate the digital transformation process, to include automating code deployments, modernize the infrastructure and security systems.

The following use case format and criteria vary, depending upon the nature of the work, but rooted in each are conventional components such as defining the problem and outlining actions. For the purpose of this chapter, I have selected criteria associated with only a few of the possible use cases. The list of other use cases can be found in chapters two and three. It seems logical to start with the migration use case as it requires an inventory or discovery of the current infrastructure, applications, and skills. The inventory results will inform all other use cases.

Selected in this chapter are those efforts and mindset that:

- Build the network pathways and security platforms required by all use cases.

- Reduce costs, once the transition is completed.

- Repurpose staff time toward more strategic initiatives.

- Provide insight into high-value cloud uses, such as improving the software development process, predictive analytics or machine learning models.

- Automate with new provisioning tools and improve self-service capabilities.

- Provide an assessment of professional services needed, such as one-time tasks during the cloud transition.

- Highlight that application development improvements in the cloud are as much about improving its methodology as it is the use of new tools.

The use case criteria outlined in this chapter enable:

- Creating a cloud migration approach

- Developing an integration strategy (applications, data, servers)

- Assessment of needed cloud vendor skills

- Pulling it all together with the creation or update of a comprehensive master data management platform, to include:
  - Data cleansing and preparation requirements
  - Cloud operational capabilities
    - Back up
    - Primary storage
    - Archiving

- ▪ Business Continuity
- Analytics platform
  - o Recreating an application development methodology with new cloud tools
  - o Making security pervasive to the entire hybrid environment
  - o Leveraging cloud network tools to ensure a high quality of service for all uses
  - o Building machine learning models
  - o Endorsing and using a cost management system

The big story when determining the implementation sequence of cloud use cases, rest with recognizing the relationship between each. There are large overlaps in tools, functionality, and dependencies which can complicate the cloud transition project schedule of events. Such as:

- Security functionality exists with network infrastructure, databases, master data platforms, and application development. Security tools used to encrypt data could come from within the database, network appliance capability or within storage devices.
- Network acceleration tools must take into account the needs of specific software application performance requirements.
- Migration tools are closely coupled to moving just the data, servers or applications. Migration platforms rely heavily on data, as such they are tied at the hip to the master data management platform.
- Distinguishing between related components can be difficult, such as:
  - o Databases
  - o Database management services
  - o Business Analytics

Use Case 1: Migrating Data, Applications and Servers to the Cloud

Of course, the goal is to have a seamless and non-disruptive cloud migration. Not unlike any large-scale project, a smooth migration requires a well thought out plan. Migrations can fail for a multitude of reasons, ranging from poor planning to poor execution. Most cloud migrations are risky. If considering the cloud transition as a series of projects, then, as mentioned in chapter two, traditional project management methodologies apply to help ensure success. Using a structured project management approach will be useful to all use cases but particularly that of developing a migration strategy.

Good project management with a stepwise execution can accelerate the journey to the cloud.

What will be needed:

- A deep understanding of your current systems
- Cloud migration experience to speed the process
- Knowledge of the cloud architecture

One can broadly define the migration components as:

- Servers
- Databases
- Applications
- Just the data (the foundation of all workloads)

Migration considerations include:

- Minimizing business disruption during the migration and remaining fully operational during the transition
- Synchronizing production workload data changes and upgrades during a migration
- Developing a fail-safe rollback/exit plan

- Zero risk of data loss

- Considering the use of purpose-built products

- Recognizing there are plenty of items that can fall through the cracks (i.e., DNS routing, syncing AD & LDAP, identity systems)

- How to accelerate the migration process and cloud-related benefits

- Building the new cloud environment to scale efficiently and securely

- Protecting the data with secure file transfer protocols (SFTP)

- Get a few easy wins

- Conduct a workload architecture assessment

- Identify end of life dates and consider not moving those applications

- Conduct a fit-gap analysis to determine the best fit for cloud instances and storage configurations.

- Consider retiring storage arrays and move the data sets to cloud storage

- Governance and change management procedures are critical

- Create replication schedules that fit your need based upon the type and size of the data

- Data transfer involves the collection, replication, and transfer of datasets within or outside a company (i.e., business partners). As large sets of data can take an extended time to transfer, performance becomes key. Automation will also be key to simplify and quicken the process.

- Care is necessary when setting up data transfer processes to ensure it has the necessary compliance information (i.e., time, destination, size).

Primary Rehosting or Replatforming Choices

1. **Lift and shift: Migrate and re-host applications and workloads as an IaaS solution.**

   That is, move the existing premise-based application to the cloud with little or no modifications. Simply spin up a cloud server instance, storage, network connection and move the workload to the cloud. The user will likely not know the application lives in a different location and as such this option is the least disruptive. The lift and shift option is also likely the lowest cost option to move legacy applications. However, it also does not offer enhancements otherwise found with newer applications.

   Also, migrating the legacy application to a cloud-based IaaS platform will not relieve the staff of application maintenance or most system administration duties.

2. **Completely rewrite the application as a cloud-native application.**

   Move the users and start anew. Clearly, this is the most expensive and staff intensive option but would result in improved functionality, if needed. If additional functionality is not needed, simply leave the workload on site and spend your efforts elsewhere.

3. **Replace it with an SaaS offering**

   Replacing a premise-based application with a SaaS offering would be chosen in order to derive more value from the investment. Functional enhancements such as improved usability, better performance, specific functionality, streamlining process improvement or stronger integration with other applications.

   If your functional needs can be met by an existing vendor supported application, then a SaaS (Software as a Service) alternative is the best option. The SaaS option also allows your team to step away from the application's daily management duties and focus on other tasks. It will be the most disruptive option; however, it will likely have the most value.

4. **Leave the application in the data center and set an end-of-life date**

Setting an end of life date for legacy applications while building or buy the next generation application, is only indirectly related to a cloud transition discussion.

Yes, replacing the legacy application with another that better meets current needs, is a good choice, but an equal benefit comes after the legacy application is decommissioned, as costs and complexity of running the older application are removed. Choosing to remove applications from the IT portfolio is more fundamentally valuable than deciding where it physically lives (i.e., premise data center or in the cloud). If end-of-life is set for an application, results include reduced staff support time, hardware and licensing reductions and an improved user interface.

Current Environment Inventory

An important first step to analyzing workloads is to gain clear visibility into the current infrastructure inventory. Consider using a portion or all of the tables in the appendix to help collect and organize the results of your discovery effort. They consist of the following categories:

Data Collection Groups

- Group A: Current Primary services and portfolio delivery model

- Group B: Current Individual Activity Costs

- Group C: Current Business Environment

Group A: Primary Service and Portfolio Delivery Model

- Table A1: IT services delivery model

- Table A2: IT service portfolio

- Table A3: Key stakeholder needs

- Table A4: Software application rationalization-maturity assessment

Group B: Individual Activity, Their Drivers and Costs

- Table B1: All activities associated with current service delivery model
- Table B2: Infrastructure maturity assessment
- Table B3: Electronic storage
- Table B4: Server and virtualization software
- Table B5: Databases
- Table B6: Software licenses
- Table B7: Security
- Table B8: Data management
- Table B9: Business continuity
- Table B10: Data Center operation
- Table B11: Skills assessment
- Table B12: Unused capacity
- Table B13: Risk assessment

Group C: Current Business Environment

- Table C1 Current outsourcing arrangements and costs
- Table C2 Current and planned projects
- Table C3 Current consulting arrangements and costs
- Table C4 Current vendor commitments and annual expenses
- Table C5 Summary of current operations
- Table C6 Current equipment installed base/Capital Expenditure (CapEx) cost
- Table C7 Overall costs of current service delivery model

Tool Selection

Proper tool selection is important and can simplify and automate the migration. When learning the types of cloud-based tools available, the following should be considered.

- Purpose-built appliances are devices available to assist with migration and integration across multiple physical platforms.

- Automated tools are valuable to speed discovery and helpful when making prioritization decisions. Discovery tools, though expensive, will also help better understand workloads. Consider leasing discovery tools to gather items such as server and storage usage, performance capability along with capacity assessments.

- The cloud giants offer tools to coordinate data transfer. These tools do not accrue a cloud fee; however the resources they consume do (storage, compute, in/out data flow, etc.)

- Cloud hubs track migration progress from multiple locations.

- Tools that automatically replicate servers.

- Management consoles help observe potential failures and trends

- Use specific, dedicated network connections during the migration process (i.e., AWS DirectConnect)

- Use data sync products that handle encryption, scripts, and network performance.

- Informatica Cloud for AWS RDS is an example of a migration tool from on premise-based databases to AWS RDS.

Vendor Migration Services

Another important decision is giving strong consideration toward hiring a cloud vendor that has developed a proven migration methodology.

Get help to:

- Select the best tools and practices
- Assist with activities performed only once.
- System integrator skills with proper certifications (i.e., Microsoft, SAP, Oracle)

Cloud giants and their partners have a set of tools and services to help make the move, ranging from:

- Compute platforms with several storage types
- A wide selection of databases and database services
- Bandwidth capacity
- Security tools to ensure the transfer process has the needed integrity
- Cost calculators to estimate costs
- Appliances and techniques to capture large amounts of data, such as:
  - Transfer products that have multiple capabilities (storage management, computing capacity, security, monitoring)
  - Suitcase size appliances shipped to your site that accept your data, then physically shipped to the cloud giant
  - For larger amounts of data (i.e., data center shut downs), transport vehicles designed to come to the data center, transfer the data and return to the cloud giants' sites to upload all of the data to the cloud
  - Enable migrations between different databases. i.e., Oracle to Microsoft or Oracle to AWS Aurora

Use Case 2: Developing a Cloud Integration Platform

I get a kick out of how trade journals are suggesting the future of information technology platforms with be in the form of a hybrid cloud! And they report, the hybrid cloud will continue to lead the way for most cloud strategies! Well, what amuses me about the observation is that it really isn't very insightful. All CIOs know they don't have a choice but to live in both worlds for a long time. The transition can't occur overnight; so, of course, it will be a hybrid environment for years to come!

Integration solutions have evolved from the day when only one enterprise system existed (i.e., ERP) to include additional enterprise-wide systems, such as a CRM's and SCM's. Information technology architectures have strived and accomplished integration for decades, so the cloud does not introduce a new concept. However, the cloud does have new tools to speed the integration process. They can connect all applications in batch processing or real-time, in the cloud and/or on the premise. The Microsoft integration set of services provide a good example of the types of tools available.

The integration design is not a once and done process as data, and its use is constantly changing. Making integration pervasive throughout the architecture has to be a top goal. The goal should be to create and streamline complex integration flows quickly and efficiently.

Numerous approaches exist when developing integration systems however they all become deeply entwined within other key architecture components (databases, workflow processes, applications, and APIs). Master data management platforms are also closely coupled with integration systems as data preparation, and data quality are important to both architectural components. As you strive for convergence, syncing of technology, processes, and people, the integration platform becomes the heart of the effort.

Multiple partner types, within and outside the company, along with many developers, will be heavy users and have a stake in the integration design. Because integration is important to so many, integration platforms can also assist in building a collaborative relationship between IT and line of business units. And this is a strategic win!

Application integration is the blending and fine tuning of data and processes between multiple but separate systems. It uses middleware to sync and translate cloud connectors (or APIs) to accomplish its goal.

Design components that will help with Integration include:

- Paying attention to uniform API management
- Embracing open source standards
- Revisiting every component and layer in the stack
- Point to point integrations are not manageable
- Aggregate and federate data is necessary to obtain data consistency and synchronization, hence strong data governance is required
- Ease of runtime management
- When possible, use pre-built and reusable components, such as cloud-based integration hubs

Use Case 3: Preparing for Cloud Storage

Electronic storage, one of the sweet spots in the cloud.

Outline to help prepare for cloud storage:

- Steps to create a storage sourcing strategy
- Spending more time at the 'wisdom' layer
- Reviewing your current storage environment, with an eye toward design, costs, and usage; with the latter as the key.
- Conducting several concurrent actions to obtain multiple goals
- Activities and thoughts to ponder as you build your cloud storage strategy
- Elements of a reliable, secure and retrievable storage system

Steps to Create a Storage Sourcing Strategy

It is clear, as a new service delivery model, the cloud has many promises, many of which are being delivered every day. From quicker application delivery times to cheaper compute and storage capability. Not to mention faster time to value with the use of cloud-based development tools.

But of all the cloud opportunities, storage is one of the sweet spots as it addresses several areas of concern across several different use cases.

At the same time though, cloud storage adoption rates for tier one services are lagging behind. Sure, lots of data is being stored in the cloud, but not much of it is for applications like ERP systems.

Concerns such as day to day security protection of the data, along with the needed ability to retain control of the data are a couple of headwinds pushing back at allowing mission-critical data finding the cloud as its primary home.

Spending More Time at the 'Wisdom' Layer

But the quicker you can put in place the basic cloud storage infrastructure that serves tier-one applications, regardless of where they live, the sooner you can move up the value chain, you remember….data, information, knowledge, wisdom. You know, spend more time with the analytics, not the plumbing. Data must be analyzed to be successful.

However, simply diving into the cloud storage environment without a strategy is unwise. Before developing a strategy and beginning the rollout of specific cloud storage use cases, it's worth setting a few goals. Developing these goals could be obtained by addressing at least three key areas. Actions you could take include:

- Review your current storage environment with an eye toward design, costs, and usage, with the latter being the key.
- Develop a clear understanding of the cloud marketplace (storage appliance vendors beyond the cloud giants).
- Develop specific cloud storage uses cases that solve more than one problem concurrently.

Review your current storage environment with an eye toward design, costs, and usage, with the latter as the key.

Let's start with the usage portion of data. A large opportunity exists here, as it is likely a lot of your storage footprint is seldom retrieved and is very old. If so, before you assess the design and cost issues for this data or any other data, possibly you should delay your new cloud storage implementation while you attempt to reconcile your corporate retention policies with the data you currently store on site. Beware though—the process will take a while!

You could argue it is easier and cheaper to simply sweep all your data under the carpet, regardless of its value. That is, don't bother trying to reduce the total volume of data. Instead, throw it up in the cloud and get on with developing specific cloud storage use cases centered around important applications that actually use critical data. After all, cloud storage is cheap, right? That's the argument my wife and I used over the years. Simply pack everything we own and we will sort through it after we relocate to our new home...err!

Besides, not many really understand retention policies anyway, nor are we humans good at routine housekeeping. Right?

Regardless of how you approach data cleansing and adherence to company retention policies, you have data design, costs, and actual usage issues to address, as you create a cloud storage architecture.

The usual suspects that should be part of your storage design include use cases such as:

- Backup/recovery
- Business continuity
- Archiving
- Specific applications like File Shares
- Test/Dev

Let's look at the opportunities that surround several of these use cases. Better yet, what if you could lay the groundwork that lends itself to accomplishing several storage issues?

Conducting several concurrent actions to obtain multiple goals:

- Leverage cloud storage appliances for both disaster recovery and routine backup solutions. That is, integrate backup and disaster recovery designs, for example, implement a solution with real-time and continuous image replication, i.e., automatically synchronize the data between two physical locations such that your systems are up-to-date and able to failover or switch to the cloud at any given time.

- Reduce latency by improving storage optimization with multi-tier caching.

- Repurpose existing storage gear by archiving data with slower storage retrieval requirements.

- Enable workload location independence by uncoupling applications and data locations.

- Improve faster data replication and enable quicker restores with the use of disk-based backup appliances and data deduplication technology.

- Create your disaster recovery design so you don't have to touch it again. That is, take the risk out of keeping both primary and secondary images in sync on a day to day basis, while also reducing the dependency on your staff to restore systems, at time of disaster.

Activities and thoughts to ponder as you start to build your cloud storage strategy:

- Discuss with the data business owner the importance and growth characteristics of their data and create matrices that map upcoming needs and storage growth requirements.

- Review the status of the software application the data serves. Possibly the application is at the end of its life cycle. Knowing this would affect how much time you spend redesigning the storage environment it serves.

- Assess your current unused storage capacity (remember, it's the most expensive kind of storage!).

- Assess the value of your current data warehouse as it serves structured data. Did it ever met the hub and spoke design intended to integrate dissimilar databases?

- Determine how you integrate your data warehouse with Hadoop.

- Decide where you should house the Hadoop distribution. Say "the cloud," please!

- Document or inventory your current environment, to include its key characteristics of (i.e., growth rate, file type, age). Actions such as;

  o Itemize the type of storage technology currently in place in your design (i.e., object storage, block storage, amount of PC

File Storage/Backup, type of cloud archiving, existing server backup solutions).

- o Index data based on criticality, i.e., tier one, tier two, tier three.

- o List different classification types, including structured and unstructured data.

- Determine your level of investment in the current storage architecture and data management environment.

- Review the basics, from an application dependency perspective, design trade-offs such as latency, performance, and redundancy.

- Facilitate the review of your current record retention policies, with an eye toward their refresh. Clear retention policies that reflect correctly balance business risks are important.

Elements of a Reliable, Secure, and Retrievable Storage System

An integrated architecture that builds upon the current storage design and the potential cloud storage offerings addresses principles such as:

- Built-in automation in the entire storage design

- Reduction of the complexity of migrating both data and applications to the cloud

- Recognition of the continued importance of the key components of structured data, data warehouses and operational stores that are used to meet performance management and ad hoc reporting needs.

- Awareness that unstructured data mining needs will be storage intensive and are best stored and mined in the cloud from the outset, e.g., activate Hadoop distributions and low-cost storage in the cloud.

- Storage mediums and equipment performance choices should be based upon usage, i.e., data that will stay at rest for long periods of time should be housed on equipment with slower retrieval capability and subsequently reduced costs.

- One that addresses data in motion and at rest.

- One that leverages public cloud for extra capacity and bursting

- Optimized from end-to-end to ensure high throughput regardless of where the application or storage physically reside.

- Ensure data is not a one-way trip to the cloud. Design both to the cloud and the premise.

I'm just saying...

- A little housekeeping goes a long way.

- A usage assessment from the outset helps.

- Communicating early and often with the application owner will pay dividends.

- A clear understanding of all storage architecture & design principles will help you build a new storage environment.

- After the housekeeping, use cases with a clear beginning and ending project dates remains the best approach.

The sooner you start, the sooner you up your game to data analytic activities and their benefits!

Hey, remember—you can't finish if you don't start.

Use Case 4: Data Management

Data Management Components

Critical Housekeeping (plumbing)
- Back up
- Primary storage
- Archive
- Business continuity

Master data platforms (Wisdom from the Data)
- Business Intelligence (software classification that automate and recommend mapping schema)
- Analytics
- Warehouse
- Data mining (unstructured data)

Working with data is a tale of two stories.

One story is that of necessary critical housekeeping tasks. Backup and archive processes must be in place to ensure the data are protected from loss. Closely coupled with protecting the data is that of maintaining business continuity. New replication software is helping to integrate the data and business functions of storing, accessing, failover, archiving and uniformity.

To start an assessment of these housekeeping tasks, ask the following questions:

- What difficulties currently exist when protecting data and operations?

- What are the key attributes of currently installed solutions?

- Can I unify data protection tasks with new replication software and techniques? And if so, what are the benefits, costs, and difficulty of implementation?

Common characteristics and requirements for all tasks include:

- A secure methodology with high availability and resiliency without business disruptions during implementation
- Acceleration tools and protocols for large data transfers
- A solution architecture with technology modernization and decommission of old software and processes (i.e., retiring magnetic tape backup solutions)
- Process improvement (i.e., automate and removal of human intervention during backup and disaster recovery operations).
- Geographically dispersed target locations

The second story when working with data is that of putting the data to work to help inform and predict, often referred to as business intelligence or analytics. The goal is to mine unstructured data to transform, organize and model data to better understand, predict and draw conclusions that identify patterns such as customer sentiment. This category also includes managing structured data with warehouses and operational stores to provide routine reports to run the business.

Because there are so many required and desired steps related to the proper management of data, a master plan is necessary. Key aspects that control both stories include:

- Policy implications (retention and compliance regulations)
- Governance actions that identify data standards and practices
- Gaps in data ownership
- Clear stewardship identification
- Transforming staff skills to build and support new ways of managing data
- Managing document flow systems

Common to all aspects of data management are:

- Clean data
- One source of the truth
- Structured approach to integration through use of APIs
- Uniform data format

The requirement to be spot on regarding meeting the business information needs of the data is important. Creating a new data management platform is costly and difficult. Getting it right is essential.

Traditional data warehouses help make sense of structured data from more than one source. Data warehouses were initially created to help off-load the operational data stores (ODS) found in transactional production systems. ODS's are a key component of large business systems like ERPs. Traditional warehouses usually have data management system functionality with query tools. Data marts are often used to further categorize data.

More on Data Housekeeping

Using the cloud as either a primary or failover repository is one of the sweet spots of the cloud. With numerous geographically dispersed data centers, the cloud is a natural fit to protect data when regional catastrophic events occur. As a primary data repository, the cloud provides high availability from anywhere in the world. The cloud has been designed to handle enterprise-level business continuity and routine data management tasks.

Disaster recovery is the technique of establishing new network paths necessary to gain access to mission-critical applications. A full disaster recovery plan will require the mission-critical applications to be preinstalled on alternative hardware. Both data and service restoration are important as revenue and reputation are at stake.

A few enterprise scale business continuity criteria include:

- Defining which systems are mission-critical

- Recovery time objective (RTO) and recovery point objective (RPO) are important benchmark requirements.

- Resource mapping and orchestration at time of disaster are part of the design

- Routine testing is time-consuming but critical. The testing must include the assurance that all critical business functions are restored.

- Day to day changes to production system configurations must be incorporated in a disaster recovery solution. Therefore, a structured change management process is important to recovery success.

New replication software now available in the cloud helps ensure data is always up-to-date and consistent. Replication software continuously duplicates data and systems on a regular basis. The software also generates redundant database copies to help improve resiliency.

An example of cloud products and functions can be found with Microsoft's cloud managed service:

- Traffic Manager-Reroutes DNS traffic

- Site Recovery-orchestrates and creates new computers and VM instances

- Active Directory replicates the premise-based AD such that user access can be authenticated

- Azure Storage to store machine images

- VPN Gateway ensures a connection between the premise and the cloud

- Virtual Network will be leveraged at time of disaster

- Replicates virtual machines to the cloud as an automated disaster recovery operation

Master Data Management (MDM): One Source of the Truth

MDM is not new, but cloud-based products are.

MDM creates one source of all critical data and includes sharing, consolidating, analyzing data and delivering it to where it is needed. Key outcomes from an MDM plan include consistent and efficient data strategies. Creating an MDM starts with data cleansing by deleting inaccurate or obsolete information and concludes with an up to date and consistent master reference. Four elements of MDM are integration, data governance, controls, and data quality. Ensuring a clear MDM plan is in place has become even more important when introducing multiple enterprise-wide software systems such as ERPs and CRMs. Integration between these systems helps synchronize the data, create common definitions and helps remove the need and cost for duplicate data. A well-synchronized MDM captures and enables continuous changes to all systems.

Investing time with MDM can:

- Improve business value from ensuring data accuracy and consistency
- Increase application performance and process efficiency
- Quicken the path to the insight the data can provide
- Better support data governance rules
- Assist in keeping data compliant with policies and regulations
- Engage data stewards
- Orchestrate across dissimilar systems
- Isolating data helps analyze it
- Provide an end to end lifecycle
- Avoid security breaches

Use Case 5: Analytics

Big data is normally defined as unstructured data as it comes in large volumes in many forms ranging from video, text, and audio and from many sources such as social media, computers, IoT, mobile devices, customers and databases.

Big data can be characterized by:

- Very large size-terabytes or petabytes
- Growing at an unmanageable rate
- Frequently changing

Big data analytics is the effort of pulling valuable information from raw data that is often large with inconsistent data types and sources.

So many members of the workforce need accurate and actionable data to successfully assess their current environment and open up new business opportunities. Increasingly, Chief Data Officers are emerging and tasked with developing an integrated view of company mined data. They are building teams that include data editors and scientists but also business line officer inclusion is also critical. Data-driven decisions that harness the data are business differentiators. A data strategy is needed and should be a business strategy that highlights opportunities and solves problems. Relevant data can move decision-making processes from learning how to prevent certain actions to actually predicting them.

There is a blending today of traditional structured data management (warehouses and operational stores) to that of new Hadoop distributions to make sense of unstructured data. Both methodologies are becoming more closely coupled to Artificial Intelligence to help make sense of the data. Open source Hadoop distributions process big data structures using many servers and are part of the Apache Software Foundation. Hadoop frameworks can ingest and process unlimited amounts of data. Cloud giants have big data platforms that have removed the platform operational tasks and allow you to develop expertise capturing, processing and analyzing your data.

Challenges include:

- Collecting data without human intervention

- Store, access and manage data efficiently

- Remove data silos

- Use software connectors or APIs to insert data into applications, reports, and dashboards

- Overcoming poor data integration, fragmented data, and disconnected data sources

- Improve poor data governance

- Define data standards

- The value of redundant data is similar to the cost of unused storage or compute capacity. None! Therefore, lifecycle management is necessary as storing data when no longer needed increases costs and liability.

- Learning how to lower the high cost of mining data and presenting it in a useable form.

- Inadequate analytical analysis specialists

Use Case 6: Content Delivery Services

Linking the cloud, applications, and users has always been important. Today, businesses operating globally with numerous locations, devices, and applications are looking to cloud services to assist. Workload dependencies require the network to perform by controlling optimization and visibility tools. The goal is to quickly design, deploy and manage a hybrid architecture that extends the existing data center into the cloud. Network delivery platforms ensure your critical applications are accessible with firewall and web accelerator capability. Increased bandwidth and (full stack) visibility is also necessary when migrating server workloads to the cloud. Real-time optimization techniques that adapt to application needs are available to maximize cloud performance during and after workload migration.

When using the public internet between cloud giants' regions, special care is needed to ensure the quality of service, such as with the use of IPsec encrypted tunnels. Storing data in multiple locations can reduce travel distances. Multi paths and split paths designs can help determine the optimal path. If a path degrades, the network can seamlessly transfer to a new path.

Let's parse the necessary criteria into three categories:

- Network design goals
- Network challenges
- Cloud network tools

Network design goals:

- Connecting people to their apps
- Ensuring everything is accessible from any location
- Improving availability, predictability and throughput performance
- Defining and reducing latency requirements
- Reducing attack surfaces

- Obtaining optimization improvements via software-defined network technologies that automate and provide zero touch provisioning
- Provide acceleration capabilities, particularly for large file migrations
- Enable comprehensive visibility of the cloud, WAN, LAN and attached devices
- Provide class of service guarantees based on content-based routing rules, cashing, auto-scaling and traffic management policies

Current network challenges include:

- Applications that are unpredictable and prone to stall with frequent database inquiries
- Bursty internet traffic
- Capacity spikes
- Bandwidth intensive applications
- Security threats
- Networks congestion during heavy use
- SLAs for internet broadband do not exist
- Hard to manage when you don't have end-to-end control
- Difficulty automating cloud security operations

Cloud Network Tools

A choice of a mix of technologies that balance security, ease of management and acceleration protocols are available. Cloud giants and vendors provide cloud visibility, optimization, connectivity, and SD-WAN functionality.

The cloud network delivery services are a collection of enterprise management functionality and network tools, such as:

- WAN optimization services that sort through MPLS, Internet or Internet VPN choices and include WAN enabled policies to simplify pathway selection and application groups and priority. Tools are also available to replace MPLS networks with SD-WAN.

- Traffic manager policies and capabilities such as load balancing compute instances (layer 4) and application (layer 7) traffic across multiple devices

- Web access accelerations protocols and services

- Quality of service (QoS) functionality

- Caching to lower latency by distributing server loads across regional centers

- DNS and IP address management

- Purpose built network appliances

- Firewalls

- Network management tools providing end to end visibility

Use Case 7: Security, Risk Management and Identity Management Systems

Cloud and on-premise security are very similar and cyber criminals have wanted to secure access and control over computer accounts for both environments since their beginnings.

All companies have been security conscious for a very long time; however, entering the cloud requires existing security platforms to be expanded. The needed outcome is to avoid a data breach when entering the cloud. Developing a consistent approach between on-premise data centers, public cloud, hybrid cloud, and private clouds will help.

When expanding into the cloud, it is necessary to build or update and deploy a comprehensive security architecture that will protect applications, data and service disruptions.

One of the challenges in building or updating a security architecture is that of evaluating the enormous number of cloud-based tools, vendors and techniques available to assist. Given this difficulty, consider finding a security partner to help navigate the choices.

Developing a shared responsibility model is a must, consisting of the customer, the cloud giant, and the cloud vendor marketplace.

To meet the cloud giants' responsibilities, they have extensive internal controls to protect their core services and infrastructure. They have taken their responsibility seriously and you will be envious. All members of the cloud giants have placed security as a top criterion, both in design and operating practices. The cloud giants also have customer tools to aid in the security effort.

For the most part, the customer is responsible for its data, implementation of identity management architectures and company applications.

Cloud vendor responsibility can, if chosen, include products that build upon the cloud giants; capabilities and often can simply run as an instance on compute platforms.

Use of cloud giants and their vendor partners is critical when entering the cloud. We know risk management is a balance of protection, accessibility, cost and effective administration. Said differently, maintaining confidentiality, availability, and system performance are end goals. Though the cloud marketplace can help with the balancing act between ease of use, security, and access, it will be necessary to understand and document who is responsible for each security component.

As said, building a partnership to gain assistance with existing and emerging threats is critical. The cloud marketplace has services and products to help with everything from physical security to incident response. The cloud marketplace can help at the application level, the perimeter or anywhere in between. The delivery model can be an appliance, virtual instance or a managed service.

The cloud marketplace also has full awareness of compliance requirements. You will be impressed.

For example, their knowledge and expertise consists of:

- Ability to document events and analysis to ensure compliance requirements are met
- HIPPA, PCI, DSS, SOX, SOC2,ISO,Cobit framework, GLBA and much more
- Compliance audits for GDPR (General Data Protection Regulation)
- Incident management, escalation, and response

Other cloud security marketplace services to protect sensitive data include:

- Continuous vulnerability scanning capabilities to help ensure unauthorized access does not occur to mission-critical network and systems
- Web application security and intrusion detection
- Use of analytics, log collection, and monitoring

- Assist building a remediation plan

Building and deploying a comprehensive security architecture includes:

- Assessing the most prevalent threats
- Building an architecture that scales is resilient and flexible
- Builds or expands an IDM system to authenticate and authorize multiple trusted sources to share. This can be done either by using an existing IDM system or by building a new one consisting of cloud federated protocols.
- The ability to perform multiple threat detection functions
- Multi-factor authentication
- Endpoint protection
- Enables remote remediation functions
- Cryptojacking, phishing scams, malware, viruses protection
- Continuous monitoring
- Device-level network traffic
- Bots attacks
- Denial of service (DoS) protection
- Encryption and access control
- Develops staff that and are technology savvy in multiple areas (network and compute systems, applications, and security best practices)
- Risk assessment analysis work
- Create or expand a security operation center
- Inventory the amount and age of your web applications as they are a prime target. You may be surprised how many web applications, including their age, you have.

Use Case 8: Machine Language Modeling

Machine language is the science and means of translating data into wisdom—wisdom in its highest value; informed predictive forecasting. Machine language functionality enables the computer to learn on its own to assess trends and potential outcomes, both in real time and asynchronously. Training machine learning models to make observations can strengthen semantic enrichment.

The cloud giants will not disappoint when reviewing their open source Python technology and machine language services used to create meaningful models. Their products and service environments can either allow the use of prebuilt machine learning modules or tools to build new ones.

Creating machine learning models is not for the faint of heart. It is an iterative and complex process with the knowledge needed when selecting algorithms, frameworks and tuning it to the desired outcome.

The cloud giants' machine learning services are closely integrated with other valuable products, such as Docker container and Kubernetes provisioning tools. It also has access to workflow tools to interconnect key phases of the machine learning deployment. Understanding the flow of enterprise data requires a close relationship between analytics and machine language. Consistency in activity between both areas is important.

Potential value includes:

- Allocating resources toward machine learning work enables the ability to quickly act on information and make better decisions across the enterprise

- Solve data challenges and unlock new value in the company data

- Strengthen applications with machine learning intelligence

- Machine learning helps interpret your data

- Assists with huge data sets difficulties, structured or unstructured

- Provides predictive modeling and data mining

- Data categorization, sentiment analysis, and natural language processing

Applied examples of why to invest in machine language modeling:

- Collect customer data that highlights similar patterns that lead to developing buying preferences
- Ability to build speech models not unlike your targeted audience speaking patterns
- Machine learning models to speak and chat with customers, freeing employee time
- Deliver insights to inform the company strategy.
- Anticipate demand, based on trends
- Product recommendations based on shopper behaviors
- Connect shopping experiences
- Improve transaction monitoring

Cloud-based machine learning productivity tools, languages, frameworks, and services are numerous with built-in components, such as:

- Cognitive toolboxes to build deep learning models with support for Apache MXNet, TensorFlow algorithms, Caffe2.
- Training, tuning and hosting repositories that can receive massive data sets from multiple sources
- Provide parallelism with multiple machines including memory sharing
- Pretrained models and pre-built APIs with automated reproducibility
- Detect when devices are breaking rules
- AWS, IBM, Microsoft, and Google all offer pre-packaged machine learning services that allow you use to train, deploy, automate, and manage machine learning models and algorithms, all at a broad scale.

Action Items:

- Prepare and cleanse data for building, training and tuning models.

- Establish simulation model configuration parameters using optimization algorithms.

- Build Cognitive interfaces.

- Develop algorithms and shape inference based on your data.

- Infuse machine language into your applications.

- Build or use prebuilt machine language algorithms engines that predict behavior based on the past.

- Build or select prebuilt APIs to integrate applications and data .

- Review and consider using preconfigured industry-specific analytic solutions.

- Develop a culture of continuous modeling.

Use Case 9: Application Development in the Cloud

Building applications in the cloud are as much about changing the development methodology as it is about potentially migrating existing databases to the cloud or selecting new cloud tools. If the development environment already uses Agile, the transition will be much easier. However, if not, the effort will be one of change management more so than new tools and migration decisions.

The Agile philosophy and practice is generally baked into most cloud application development tools. Their uses are designed to use the Agile approach of short continuous code releases, iterate and incremental building. Many believe short iterative changes speeds up and makes the process more responsive to changes and testing. Following the Agile practice early in the development process can preclude missing release deadlines.

There are other related processes such as waterfall and lean (continuous improvement methodology), but some would suggest Agile is better suited to software development as it reduces development time.

In addition to considering changing development methodologies, reviewing the existing applications portfolio is critical.

An Inventory effort should include:

- List of all current applications
- List of all currently used development tools
- Current staff skills
- Determine which applications are at end-of-life
- Determine which applications are the best and most useful

When reviewing the inventory results, I suggest not focusing on the oldest applications but instead the applications that can or do provide the most value to the company.

Another important consideration is to evaluate the cloud PaaS environment (i.e., Salesforce force.com). Born-in-the-cloud, the PaaS environment is rich with tools and has numerous development platforms.

So, in short when thinking about your application development efforts and potentially the use of the cloud, consider the following broad areas of concern:

- Changing or improving your development methodology to provide a more predictable delivery cycle.
- Contrast current and cloud tools to assess which can accelerate development
- Inventory all aspects of your current development environment
- The assessment should include software development teams willingness and capability to implement a new development platform and methodology.

Important considerations:

- Differentiating between related development efforts such as:
  - Creating and publishing APIs
  - Automating infrastructure provisioning, though a container strategy is needed to help reduce errors.
  - Developing workflow automation improvements based upon user self-service
- Developing an application-centric mindset built on high availability tools, practices, and scalability.
- Documenting software development principles
- Automating repetitive tasks
- Developing mobile applications
- Creating pipelines for continuous integration and continuous deployment to drive automation (CI/CD)

- Delivering software applications, not managing infrastructure, is strategic

- The best development efforts will integrate technology, processes, and people.

- Website development use content management systems such as WordPress, Magento, Joomia, Drupal.

Use Case 10: Database Decisions

If the application is being built in the cloud, then it clearly makes sense to select from a plethora of cloud database choices.

However, when choosing whether to move premise-based databases to the cloud, several dependencies and obstacles exist.

- The application the database serves is at end-of-life

- The application supports a limited number of databases

- The effort required to convert to a new database is too time-consuming and does not deliver improved value to the application.

On the other hand, if the decision is made to move and/or build databases in the cloud, there are many tools available. Cloud giants can assist with database related services found in the cloud, such as:

- Databases with serverless capabilities (i.e., AWS Aurora and DynamoDB)

- Professional database migration services and managed database services

- Schema conversion tools

- Many fast databases, often faster than other MySQL databases

- Migration acceleration offerings

- Re-hosting tools for the application, leaving it and its database untouched

- Database encryption tools to protect RDBMs

Database items to be aware of:

- Some database actions require special attention during migration
- The need to establish connections between source and target workload or databases, ensuring the correct replication instance is selected for each migration.
- Encryption can be obtained in numerous ways. Tools used to encrypt data could be built in the database itself, or could occur at the network level or could reside in storage appliances

Possible Database management approaches and considerations:

- Database consolidation
- Schema structure, data types, and code between the source and the target database may be different and require changes before the migration.
- Use schema conversion tools to assess the size of the effort
- Cloud database migration services include continuous data replication capability; hence, a disaster recovery use case may be considered
- Mapping databases is not uncommon such as: MySQL to AWS Aurora or Microsoft SQL server to AWS RDS for SQL server or Oracle to AWS RDS for Oracle

Appendix: Data Collection Group Tables

Data Collection Groups

- Group A: Current Primary services and portfolio delivery model
- Group B: Current Individual Activity Costs
- Group C: Current Business Environment

Group A: Primary Service and Portfolio Delivery Model

- Table A1: IT services delivery model
- Table A2: IT service portfolio
- Table A3: Key stakeholder needs
- Table A4: Software application rationalization-maturity assessment

Group B: Individual Activity, Their Drivers and Costs

- Table B1: All activities associated with current service delivery model
- Table B2: Infrastructure maturity assessment
- Table B3: Electronic storage
- Table B4: Server and virtualization software
- Table B5: Databases
- Table B6: Software licenses
- Table B7: Security
- Table B8: Data management
- Table B9: Business continuity
- Table B10: Data Center operation
- Table B11: Skills assessment
- Table B12: Unused capacity
- Table B13: Risk assessment

Group C: Current Business Environment

- Table C1 Current outsourcing arrangements and costs
- Table C2 Current and planned projects
- Table C3 Current consulting arrangements and costs
- Table C4 Current vendor commitments and annual expenses
- Table C5 Summary of current operations
- Table C6 Current equipment installed base/Capital Expenditure (CapEx) cost
- Table C7 Overall costs of current service delivery model

Table A1: IT Services Delivery Model

Phases of IT Service Delivery	Purpose	Activity Measure (major effort and type of exposure)	Driver of Activity (Dept. or function)	FTE Involved	Annual Costs Direct Indirect
Design	*List Projects Underway or in the queue*				
Build and Test	*List Projects Underway or in the queue*				
Implement	*List Projects Underway or in the queue*				
Maintain					

Collecting and documenting all services enables answering the following questions, and subsequently making sound decisions regarding the cloud transition:

- What are the costs of each service delivery phase, including the relationship of each service to other activities?
- Do any of the activity drivers seem disproportionate with their value and is this worthy of future investigation?
- Which phases will substantively change in the future i.e. increase or decrease in respective costs?
- If costs are expected to significantly change, will the delivery model change?

Service Portfolio: Keeping The End Goal In Mind

Goal: Ensure the service portfolio is aligned with company business objectives.

Table A2: Service Portfolio

Service and Function	Direct Cost	Indirect Cost	Life Cycle	Further Investment Needed?

Collecting and documenting an IT department's total service portfolio enables analyzing the answers to the following questions:

- Which IT services are and which are not aligned with the company's business model?
- Which IT services seem costly?
- Which costs will be eliminated if a particular IT service is deployed in the cloud?
- Which IT services are nearing end of life and will likely be discontinued, independent to a cloud offering?
- Which current IT services require additional investments (process engineering)?
- Which services have low usage?
- Does a functional department, outside of the central IT department, champion the cloud service to be offered?

Key Stakeholder Needs

Goal: Assess the relationships among IT services and key consumers and stakeholders.

Table A3: Key Stakeholder Needs

Stakeholder	Stakeholder Need	Cost to Fulfill Need	Is Cloud an Option?

Collecting and documenting the relationship between IT services and stakeholders enables answering the following questions:

- Who are the key stakeholders and what IT services do you currently provide to them?
- What are the costs of providing each IT service?
- What are stakeholder concerns?
- Are stakeholder/customer needs currently being met?
- Does it appear that the cloud is an option for a current or upcoming stakeholder requirement?

Software Application Rationalization Maturity Assessment

Goals: Assess the current software application maturity level and measure costs associated with delivering software applications. Rationalize the corporate value and degree of business alignment of all existing applications. Identify applications with high costs relative to usage and value. Assess the cloud's readiness to support selected software applications. Highlight potential cloud candidates ready to deploy to the cloud.

Table A4: Software Application Rationalization Maturity Assessment

Application Name	Application Maturity	Name/ Owner	Life Cycle	Needed Upgrades	FTE Needed to Support Each Application	Annual Cost

To effectively analyze the current software applications inventory, the variables should be sorted in the following ways:

- By customer department (Tier 1 software applications)
- By customer department (Tier 2 software applications)
- By internal Tier 1 application (Active Directory (AD) service, Lightweight Directory Access Protocol (LDAP), etc.)
- By those that are currently virtualized software applications
- By those software applications that can be virtualized and supported by the software manufacturer

- By maturity level, i.e., where is the software application in its life cycle?

- By software applications that are known to have SaaS equivalents

Software Application Rationalization Maturity Assessment (Cont.)

Collecting and documenting all software applications enables answering the following questions:

- Which software applications have reached and/or will reach their cost and capability limits?

- Which software applications have difficult dependencies, making high-system performance challenging to obtain, i.e., which software applications are intrinsically compute-intensive?

- Are current software applications highly customized?

- Are the existing processes, which the software applications enable, complex?

- Which software applications are currently virtualized?

- Which existing and future software applications cannot be virtualized?

- Which software applications are closely coupled to each other (latency, database instance)?

- Which applications are functionally redundant or have significant overlap?

- Which software applications are critical?

- Which software applications need to be rewritten to better blend social, mobile and enterprise applications?

- Which software applications have dependencies upon a specific commute platform?

Group B: Individual Activity, Their Drivers and Costs

Goal: Categorize and establish all activities and their respective drivers and costs.

Table B1: All Activities Associated with the Current Service Delivery Model

Activity (i.e. functions and operations)	Department Owner	Activity Measure	Growth Rate	Driver of Activity (i.e. customer or internal IT operation) indicate actual service	Annual Cost	Portion of Cost that Remains even if moved to cloud?

Collecting and documenting all services enables answering the following questions:

- What is the activity's value?
- How much effort and of what type does the activity consume?
- Is it a difficult activity for your team?
- How does the activity relate to other activities?
- At what rate will the activity grow in a five-year period?
- If deemed a difficult activity, will it continue to be supported?
- Is the activity tactical or strategic to the operation?
- If the activity is critically tied to an operation, what is its usage level and how broadly does it serve other activities?
- Will the same activity be conducted in the cloud?
- Is the activity's cost proportionate to its value?

- How many full-time equivalents (FTEs) are consumed by this activity and what type of skills are consumed by the activity?

- If the activity is continued, will future capital expenditures be required to support that activity?

- Which activities are non-essential and/or expensive, time- and/or dollar-wise and/ or are labor intensive, for driving important functions?

- Which activities drive many different functions, i.e., present high value?

- Which activities have the largest strategic impact?

- Which are low-volume activities versus high-volume activities?

- Which activities offer cost comparisons to their activity frequency?

Activity Cost

- Which activity costs consume resources that cannot be tied to a business need?

- If costs are reduced in one particular area, e.g., design, are they reduced in the other areas as well? How extensive are the reductions across activities? Or do activity reductions enable diverting saved expenses –people, maintenance, or development costs – to another area of need?

- Which activities are customer-driven costs, e.g., sales, transportation and shipping, and customer service?

- Which activities require high labor expenses?

- Which costs remain in the current operation even with outsourcing?

- Which future costs are highly capital intensive, have high fixed costs, or have uncontrollable growth costs? Can dollars be better leveraged elsewhere?

- Which services can be cheaper if addressed in the cloud?

- Which in-house services also have opportunity costs associated with them?

- Where are expenses growing the most?

- Which activities drive the most indirect costs, i.e., which require disproportionate overhead costs?

- Are the indirect activities worth it?

- Will the indirect cost-intensive activity be significantly reduced or eliminated if transitioned to the cloud?

Nature of Activity

- Which activities are difficult to automate and adjust to varying demand levels?

- Which activities consume the work priorities of highly skilled personnel?

- Which activities must continue to be managed from within, by your organization, due to confidentiality?

- What are the interdependencies among activities and costs that are triggered?

- Which activities appear to be inefficient?

- Which activities are you most efficient with?

Infrastructure Maturity Assessment

Goal: Categorize all expenses; assess level of unused capacity, including areas of immediate capacity investment needed.

Table B2: Infrastructure Maturity Assessment

Activity	Maturity	Where in Life Cycle	Further Investment Needed? If so, how much?	Driver of expenses	Level of additional capacity available	Annual Cost

In order to analyze the current software applications, variables can be sorted in the following ways:

- Servers by age; refresh date; size; purpose, e.g., web front end, application server); virtualization server; operating system
- Data center expenses
- Storage by type of storage attachment, e.g., Storage Area Network (SAN) or direct attachment; storage tier; dollars per gigabyte (GB) of capacity; array; and disk costs

Electronic Storage

Goal: Assess current storage footprint size, type, cost, and usage. Also, assess for which applications does storage serve and its expected growth rate.

Table B3: Electronic Storage

Storage Type	Serves what Purpose	Criticality	Life Cycle	Cost

Collecting and documenting all of your unit's services enables you answer the following questions:

- How well prepared is the storage environment to meet current and future needs?
- What is the current storage cost?
- What are expected storage needs and their respective costs?
- How does the current design compare to likely needed design changes?

Server and Virtualization Software

Goal: Assess the current investment in server technology and its degree of virtualization.

Table B4a: Server and Virtual Management Environment

Server Purpose	Server Type	Life Cycle	Expected Growth	Cost

Table B4b: Server and Virtual Management Environment

Server Hardware Costs	Year 1	Year 2	Year 3	Year 4	Year 5
Servers (beginning of year)					
Servers that are virtualized					
Average purchase price per server					
Server purchase costs					
Server Hardware Maintenance (OpEx)					
Total Server Hardware Costs					

Table B4c: Server Costs

Server Software Costs	Licenses	Cost per License	Total License Costs
Operating System			
Windows Server			
Linux			
Virtualization			

Documenting the characteristics of all servers and their degree of virtualization enables answering the following questions:

- How well prepared is the server environment to meet current and future needs?
- How does your current reference architecture compare to needed design changes?
- What are the current server costs, including operating systems and system management tools?
- What are the server administration costs?
- What are the expected server needs and their respective costs?
- What is the cost of the installed virtualized instance environment and expected growth rate?
- What is the actual savings from virtualization?

Note: Though server virtualization clearly: increases service availability, enables consolidation, and quicker provisioning, it is unlikely actual system administration labor will be in the cloud. More likely, is the purpose of system administrator type functions to other types of tasks.

Note: In some organizations, the server administrator is a "jack of all trades," with responsibilities including applications and network and storage administration. If system administrators' responsibilities are broader than server system administration, then it is necessary to itemize these additional responsibilities. It is likely that the additional responsibilities will be required when servers are deployed on site and in the cloud. Do develop a different cost basis for virtual servers instances and physical servers and use fully burdened costs.

Consider calculating server costs as the number of administrators divided by the number of physical and virtual servers deployed. This calculation provides an administration cost per physical or virtual server instance. For a host running 10 virtual machines, the administration costs would be calculated as one physical server plus 10 virtual servers, for a total of 11 servers.

Database

Goal: Document the database environment.

Table B5: Database Environment

Type of Database	App Served	Growth Rate	DBA %	Database License Costs	Annual Costs

Collecting and documenting all database-related costs, types, and usage enables answering the following questions:

- How many database types and instances exist in both the production and development environment?
- Are database licenses being used to the fullest?
- What unit of measure is used to determine database license costs?
- When are database licenses due for renewal?
- Does the database license provide for cloud use (IaaS, PaaS, and SaaS)?
- Do you possess the correct level of database administrator (DBA) skills on staff?

Software Licenses

Goal: Assess the complexity and costs of the current software environment.

Table B6: Software License Costs

Name/Company of Software License	Unit of Measure by which License is Sold	Annual Costs	Support Costs

Collecting and documenting all of your unit's software license costs enables answering the following questions:

- How complex is the software licensing environment?
- Are you able to draw a relationship among software license costs and the software value and usage?

Security

Goal: Assess the current spending and complexity of your information systems security environment.

Table B7: Security Environment

Security Infrastructure Equipment	Cost Per Device	Total Purchase Costs	Support Costs

Note: Include expense elements such as firewalls/Virtual Private Network (VPN), data loss prevention (DLP), rights management, identity management, authentication management, encryption, antivirus software, scanning, security management, policies, and procedures.

Collecting and documenting all of company information security costs enables answering the following questions:

- Is the current level of security sufficiently providing information technology security protection?
- Which information technology services will remain on site regardless if portions of critical services are moved to the cloud?

- Are significant future investments likely and for what purpose?

Data Management

Goal: Assess the size of all data types currently stored, how much the storage operation costs, the storage footprint growth rate, and the established retention schedule.

Table B8: Data Management

Backup Operation (Data Management)	FTE in Operation	CapEx in Future	Scalability of Solution	Size (Terabyte)	Type of Data	Annual Cost

Collecting and documenting the characteristics of all corporate information and how it is managed enables asking the following questions:

- How much data is being managed?

- How is this data managed?

- How much of this managed data is critical in the event of a disaster?

- How much of this data is considered sensitive?

- What are the current retention policies, and, if adjusted to shorter periods, how much data would be reduced?

- Has the data been categorized, separating sensitive and non-sensitive data? If categorized, how much non-sensitive data exists?

- How often is the data accessed?
- Is there a cheaper technical management solution available for infrequently accessed data?

Business Continuity

Goal: Develop a clear disaster recovery process understanding in terms of costs, exposure, automation, and areas of potential improvement.

Table B9: Business Continuity

DR of Business Continuity	Difficulty to Maintain	Costs	Recovery Time	Complexity

Collecting and documenting the corporate business continuity model enables answering the following questions:

- Were the results of the last disaster recovery exercise acceptable?
- At the time of the last disaster recovery exercise, to what degree was the recovery process dependent upon your staff's involvement?
- What is the cost of the disaster recovery model?
- Do you manage mission-critical or sensitive data using the same technology as the balance of your data?

Data Center Operations

Goal: Assess the costs, effort, and value of running your own data center.

Table B10: Data Center Operations

Operations Conducted in the Data Center	Capital Equipment	Capital Equipment Costs	FTE Involved	Refreshment Date

Collecting and documenting data regarding your data center operations enables answering the following questions:

- How much does the entire data operation cost annually?
- What is the size of your refresh budget and is it appropriately sized for equipment such as UPSs, power generators, battery backup, air conditioners, file servers, storage equipment, and tape backup equipment?
- Is there any automation that could be implemented to allow the repurposing of operations staff?
- Is there an unused data center available and, if so, how long could that space prove adequate, given your growth rate?
- Can a relationship be drawn among selected applications costs and operations costs and their data center-related costs?

Staff Skills Assessment – Current

Goal: Assess current staff skills and how they are utilized.

Table B11a: Staff Skills Assessment – Current

Job Family Name	Job Name	By Department	By Activity	Annual Cost
				List of positions and how they are shared among functions

Collecting and documenting current staff skills enables answering the following questions:

- How many FTEs are involved in the central IT operation?
- What are the skills break down of current staff, by job family?
- What activities are they involved in?
- What percentage is involved in operations versus development? Note: Pay particular attention to system administrators; often they function as jacks-of-all-trades, spending time on much more than just system administrative activities.

Staff Skills Assessment – Future

Goal: Assess future staff skills and department size requirements.

Table B11b: Future Staff Skills and Department Requirements

	Type	Purpose/ Activity	Annual Cost
Skills Needed (Current Service Delivery Model)			
Skills Surplus (Current Service Delivery Model)			
Skills avoided with movement to the cloud			
New skills required with movement to the cloud			

Collecting and documenting current staff skills enables answering the following question: If the current support and development model were maintained, how would staffing needs change during the next four years?

Assessing Unused Capacity

Goal: List the information infrastructure areas that have unused capacity.

Table B12: Assessing Unused Capacity (Equipment, Software Licenses, FTEs)

Operation	Size of Current Operation	Excess Capacity	FTE Involved	Criticality of Service Provided

Assessing unused capacity enables answering the following questions:

- Is your staff fully utilized?

- Which specific employees are performing task functions that should be repurposed?

- Do software licenses use units of measure that enable their contrast to actual utilization?

Risk Assessment

Goal: Assess and document areas in which the current operation presents a risk of operations, failure, and/or cost overruns.

Table B13: Risk Assessment

Nature of Risk	Impact of Risk	Options Available to Mitigate Risk	Costs of Each Option

Assessing enterprise risk enables answering the following questions:

- Which risks exist?
- Are these risks significant?
- Do these risks require immediate attention?

Table Group C: Current Business Environment Current Outsourcing Arrangements And Costs

Goal: Assess service areas previously outsourced.

Table C1: Current Outsourcing Arrangements

Activity	Annual Cost Avoided If In Cloud?

Collecting and documenting all outsourcing contracts enables answering the following questions:

- Are current outsourcing contracts serving their intended purpose?
- Will any of the current outsourced contracts expire soon?
- How are the outsourced services related to the current and potential service delivery methods?

Current And Planned Projects

Goal: Assess the size, planned outcomes, and costs of current and planned projects.

Table C2: Current and Planned Projects

Project Name	Skills Needed	Project Cost

Collecting and documenting all projects enables answering the following questions:

- Are current projects properly aligned with corporate business objectives?
- Can any current or planned projects be reassessed if using a cloud offering is acceptable?

Current Consulting Arrangements And Costs

Goal: Assess the rationale for establishing prior consulting arrangements.

Table C3: Assess Consulting Arrangements and Costs

Consultant Type (Skill)	Purpose / Project / Activity	Annual Cost Avoided if in Cloud?

Collecting and documenting all of your unit's services enables answering the following questions:

- Where are consulting dollars spent?
- Will current consulting dollars be reduced with a cloud-based model?
- What skills and subsequent value does the current outsourcing provide?

Current Vendor Commitments and Annual Expenses

Goal: Assess how well current vendor contracts are leveraged and for what purpose.

Table C4: Vendor Management

Consultant Type (Skill)	Purpose / Project / Activity	Annual Cost Avoided if in Cloud?

Collecting and documenting all vendor-related costs enables addressing the following items:

- Identify vendors with whom you conduct the most business
- Assess opportunities to consolidate vendor business partnerships
- Assess how well current vendors are leveraged

Summary of Current Service Delivery Model Costs

Goal: Enable a high-level view of all major cost elements, as they relate to the current service delivery model.

Table C5: Summary Of Current Service Delivery Model Costs

Design	Build and Test	Deploy	Operate	Criticality of Service Provided
Overhead/ Management				
Capital Costs				
Operating Costs				
Business Applications				

Glossary

activity based costing. An accounting system of assigning costs to products by taking indirect costs into consideration, for instance staff expenses and salaries.[45]

agile. A method of incremental software development that is an alternative to traditional project management, and which prioritizes collaboration with customers and swift response to change over sticking to a plan and contract negotiation.[8]

application program interface. A standard set of requests a software program makes of another program, to perform specific functions, such as accessing a file.[68]

authentication. A security measure, a process of determining proof of user identity before data or software can be accessed.[94]

automation capability. The potential for a system or a function, for instance, a production assembly line, to be automatically programmed and performed mechanically.[33]

automated and scalable infrastructure. Systems, hardware, and programs designed to automatically continue to function well while anticipating change in size of data processed or user growth.[35]

bare metal servers. A computer system or network in which a virtual machine is installed directly on hardware, such as a hard disk, rather than within the host operating system.[82]

business alignment. Correspondence between the goals of a business and the requirements regarding information technology in said business; to achieve business alignment, there needs to be effective communication between IT managers and executives.[81]

business continuity. The processes and procedures an organization puts in place to ensure that essential functions can continue during and after a disaster or problem.[18]

capital expenditures. Money spent by a business or organization on acquiring or maintaining fixed assets, such as land, buildings, and equipment, including hardware or software.[108]

cloud broker. A third-party individual or business that acts as an intermediary between the purchaser of a cloud computing service and the sellers of that service.[92]

cloud delivery model. Modes of data delivery (storage and access) for end users via different types of cloud service models, including SaaS, PaaS, and IaaS.[41]

cloud deployment model. A specific type of cloud environment utilized by a business, primarily distinguished by ownership, size, and access; the four types are public, private, hybrid, and community models.[117]

cloud layers. Functional components of cloud computing programming that interact in a sequence, one after the other, while only having to communicate with the layers directly above and below it in its sequence.[83]

cloud management and migration tools. The software and technologies designed for operating and monitoring applications, data and services residing in the cloud.[9]

cloud marketplace. an online storefront operated by a cloud service provider.[74]

cloud platform. An underlying computer system that lets developers write applications that run in the cloud, or use services provided from the cloud, or both.[24]

cloud transition strategy. A long-term business plan for moving certain services, applications, data, and other resources from on-premise data centers or local servers to networked cloud-based data storage and applications, which increases flexibility, scalability, and speed of operations.[29]

compute capability. An ability to process information and run programs defined by a major revision number and a minor revision number; devices with the same major revision number are of the same core architecture.[39]

consumption based pricing model. A system of payment for service providers, including those who provide cloud storage services or data services, wherein a customer is charged a set price per units of the resource used.[91]

cost management system. A form of management accounting that allows a business to predict impending expenditures to help reduce the chance of going over budget.[119]

critical IT services. Any device, system, or process whose disruption or failure will result in a collapse of business operations, because all related functions stop working; sometimes these are called mission critical systems.[105]

CRM - Customer Relationship Management. Practices, strategies and technologies that companies use to manage and analyze customer interactions and data throughout the customer lifecycle, with the goal of improving business relationships with customers.[30]

data archiving. The process of moving data that is no longer actively used to a separate data storage device for long-term retention.[85]

data deduplication appliance. A program that reduces storage needs by eliminating redundant data.[40]

data warehouse. A large store of data accumulated from a wide range of sources within a company and used to guide management decisions.[67]

databases. A collection of information that is organized so that it can easily be accessed, managed, and updated.[53]

database licenses. A form of protection granting third parties access to intellectual property on one's database when the database owner is not the copyright holder; a database license also grants legal copyright-style status to unique or original collections of data.[64]

data center operations. The workflow and processes that are performed within a data center, such as infrastructure operations, security processes, power and cooling, and management.[48]

data management. An administrative process that ensures information is accessible and reliable by means of acquiring, validating, storing, and processing that information.[19]

data mining. Analyzing large amounts of data, such as on databases or data input to content aggregates, and summarizing and picking out data that is useful to increase revenue or cut costs.[36]

data portability. A feature of cloud computing that enables re-use of data components, or components of processable information, across different applications.[65]

data portability clause. A portion of the SLA that provides clear instruction as to how quickly your data will be returned and in what format, and how input and received data can be used.[104]

DBaaS. Database-as-a-Service (DBaaS) is a service that is managed by a cloud operator (public or private) that supports applications, without the application team assuming responsibility for traditional database administration functions.[97]

depreciation schedule. An accounting procedure for determining the amount of value left in a piece of equipment.[99]

elasticity. or: the ability of an IT infrastructure to rapidly expand or cut back on services and total capacity, proportional to the needs of end users, without harming the infrastructure's stability, security, or performance.[75]

electronic storage. (1) A means of saving digital or waveform data via magnetically charged platters in hard disks, microchips in Solid State Drives, magnetic tape, or on cloud drives accessible from the internet.[113] (2) Any medium that can be used to record information electronically. Examples include hard disks, magnetic tapes, compact discs, videotapes, and audiotapes.[59]

Encryption. A method of securing data that changes the data into an unreadable code, and requires a password or key to make the data readable again.[10]

equipment depreciation costs. The expense stemming from the breakdown of equipment such as computer hardware; that is, the expense that comes as the resource is used up each financial quarter.[6]

ERP - Enterprise Resource planning. Business process management software that allows an organization to use a system of integrated applications to manage the business and automate many back office functions related to technology, services and human resources.[11]

exit strategies. A means for a business owner to cash out of an investment; this can include a merger & acquisition, an initial public offering, selling to a buyer, or liquidation of assets.[121]

file sharing. The public or private sharing of computer data or space in a network with various levels of access privilege.[77]

fixed costs. Expenses, such as rent, that stay constant in the short term regardless of levels of sales, profits, or variations production costs.[1]

FTE. Full-time equivalent, a unit measuring productivity comparable across different contexts.[20]

Hadoop. A free, Java-based programming framework that supports the processing of large data sets in a distributed computing environment.[86]

high availability capabilities. A system or component that is continuously operational for a desirably long length of time.[78]

hybrid cloud. This deployment model helps businesses to take advantage of secured applications and data hosting on a private cloud, while still enjoying cost benefits by keeping shared data and applications on the public cloud.[27]

hypervisor. A program that lets multiple operating systems share a single hardware host in a way that each operating system appears to have the host's processor, memory, and other resources; this is done by creating and running multiple virtual machines.[103]

IaaS. Infrastructure as a Service (IaaS) is a form of cloud computing that provides virtualized computing resources over the Internet.[95]

identity management. A broad administrative area that deals with identifying individuals in a system (such as a country, a network, or an enterprise) and controlling their access to resources within that system by associating user rights and restrictions with the established identity.[56]

indirect overhead costs. Initial costs not directly associated with the production of goods and services; for example, administrative salaries or legal expenses.[4]

information security. The protection of information systems, including databases, against unauthorized access to information (hacking), or unauthorized and illegal modification of information, and protection against denial of service attacks (DDOS attacks) which prevent legitimate users from accessing information.[63]

integrated architecture. A software structural system that encompasses all of the software elements, the relationships between the elements and the user interfaces to those elements.[62]

integration hubs. A data integration hub architecture means data sources are not strictly linked to destinations one-to-one, allowing applications to publish once but effortlessly support one-to-many consuming applications; for example, publishing a picture simultaneously on many social media sites with a single upload.[42]

interoperability. The level of compatibility between two or more dissimilar systems, which determines the ease with which they'll work together.[80]

IT job classification system. A method of categorizing IT jobs into families based on the nature and complexity of the work in any given job; these classifications are not based on specific tasks, but rather on the role, level, and market-based salary range of the given job.[106]

IT service maturity model. A methodology used to develop an organization's software creation process, which describes a five-level evolutionary path of increasingly organized processes, specifically IT services such as the maintenance of software systems, the operation of information systems, the management and maintenance of networks or mainframes, or the provision of contingency services.[61],[50]

IT service portfolio. (1) An index of all the IT service desk services that are currently available to end users (customers), as well as a description of services presently in planning or development stages, and services that have since been retired.[55] (2) An exhaustive list of IT services that an organization offers to its employees or customers, regardless of where they are in their life cycle (i.e. planning, development, production, retired). The Service Portfolio includes the service pipeline, a service catalog, and a list of retired services.[7]

labor intensive. A high ratio of labor costs (for example, workforce numbers or energy output) to production of any good or service.[46]

microprocessor. An integrated circuit that contains all the functions of a central processing unit of a computer; sometimes called a logic chip.[57]

Multi-tenant software. A software program or application designed to serve multiple customers, or "tenants", from a single instance of the software, with each customer's data invisible to the other users.[93]

NOSQL. Non-relational database for unstructured data--a database that stores and retrieves data using methods other than tabular relations.[58]

object-oriented tools. A programming language model or software and computing tools organized around <u>objects</u> rather than actions and data rather than logic.[76]

on demand. A pricing model in which computing resources and services are only made available to the customer as needed.[87]

operating expenditures. Routine and continuous expenses (such as maintenance, utility costs and staff salaries).[2]

operating systems. The software that supports a computer's basic functions, such as scheduling tasks, executing applications, and controlling peripherals, which allows the user to communicate with the computer without knowing programming languages. Popular Operating Systems include Windows Vista, Ubuntu, and Mac OS X.[37]

outsourcing. The corporate practice of contracting with another company for a specific service.[47]

PaaS. Platform as a Service is a category of cloud computing that provides a platform and environment to allow developers to build applications and services over the internet.[44]

pay as you go. Relating to a system of paying debts or meeting costs as they arise.[110]

pay per use basis. An SaaS model in which the end user pays a subscription fee for a service, on a per-usage basis, every time the software is used.[5]

premise-based environment. As opposed to a cloud-based environment, a premise-based environment has all systems and data available on location and under local control and maintenance, but cannot utilize cloud processing.[38]

premise-based information technology operation. A system wherein hardware for information technology, such as servers, routers, and cables, are installed on location, or on the premises of, a given company or corporation; this is in contrast to cloud-based operation.[34]

proof of concept. A demonstration that shows the real-world application of previously theoretical ideas; a prototype can be proof of concept.[49]

pricing models. Systems or algorithms for determining the price of a product or service.[122]

private cloud. The most secure model of cloud deployment, in which hosting is built and maintained for a specific client, and the server infrastructure is either on-premise or in a secure third-party location; because data is privately managed, it is called the private cloud model.[27]

public cloud. A model of cloud deployment in which services and infrastructure are provided to various clients, and the hardware is not located on premises for the end-user clients; Google services, such as Google Docs, are an example of a public cloud.[27]

qualitative benefits. Returns on an investment that are not measurable in a monetary or other objective, numerical way.[98]

quantitative benefits. Returns on an investment that are objectively measurable; for example, monetary gain.[98]

ready built web applications. Ready to use database-driven websites coded by professionals.[115]

reference architecture. A document or set of documents to which a project manager or other interested party can refer for best practices.[118]

resiliency. The ability of a server, network, storage system, or an entire data center, to continue operating even when there has been an equipment failure, power outage or other disruption.[90]

retention schedule. A policy that defines how long data items must be kept and provides disposal guidelines for how data items should be discarded.[28]

risk assessment. an evaluation of potential variables and hazards that might negatively impact a business, and preparation for meeting those challenges. Risk is calculated by assigning a number based on the probability the hazard will occur.[72]

ROI – return on investment. A ratio calculating profitability by measuring value gained compared to the level of expenditure.[32]

SaaS. Software as a Service is a software delivery method which allows data to be accessed from any device with any browser connected to the internet.[101]

RTO (recovery time objective). The maximum tolerable length of time that a computer, system, network, or application can be down after a failure or disaster occurs.[88]

SAN. A high-speed network of storage devices that also connects those storage devices with servers.[13]

software application rationalization-maturity assessment. An evaluation of software or software features by means of: selecting your applications based on business need and prioritizing related actions, effectively managing the value of both existing and proposed applications, and monitoring changing priorities and application value in real time, continually reviewing and adjusting as necessary. This is in regard to costs and usefulness of each application in its life cycle.[66]

software licenses. A legally binding agreement that specifies the terms of use for an application and defines the rights of the software producer and of the customer, or end-user, of the program.[107]

server. A server is a computer that provides data to other computers. It may serve data to systems on a local area network (LAN) or a wide area network (WAN) over the Internet. Many types of servers exist, including web servers--which provide access to websites based on HTTP requests from clients (web browsers)--mail servers, and file servers.[25]

service delivery model. The specific methods and regulations of sending an IT organization's services and products to end users, formulated by said organization, based on identified end user and provider needs, established partnerships, and resources.[23],[71]

service level agreement. A contract between a service provider and its end users (customers) that documents what services the provider will furnish.[96]

single sign on. A session/user authentication process that permits a user to enter one name and password in order to access multiple applications.[114]

software application development cycle. A series of steps that provide a model for the development and long-term management of an application or piece of software; these steps are training, requirement & design, construction, testing, and release.[109]

sourcing strategy. Or: an approach to supply chain management that formalizes the way information is gathered and used so that an organization can leverage its consolidated purchasing power to find the best possible values in the marketplace.[89]

spot pricing. The price at which a commodity could be transacted (bought and sold) and delivered on right now, "on the spot."[51]

SQL - structured query language. The standard language for relational database management systems, used to communicate with a database.[102]

SSAE 16 Type II (formally SAS 70). A compliance audit regulating SOC 1 reporting standards for accountants regarding service management.[60]

storage architecture. Methods of creating hierarchies or sequences to grants and withhold user access to stored data.[111]

storage arrays. A method for storing information on multiple devices.[73]

storage capacity. The maximum amount of data that can be held by a piece of hardware, a server, or a network of computers; storage capacity is often measured in bytes (kilobytes, gigabytes, or terabytes).[26]

storage footprint. The amount of physical space a particular unit of hardware or software occupies.[52]

structured data. Structured data refers to information with a high degree of organization, such that inclusion in a relational database is seamless and readily searchable by simple, straightforward search engine algorithms or other search operations; whereas unstructured data is essentially the opposite.[16]

tape backup system. The ability to periodically copy the contents of all or a designated amount of data from its usual storage device to a tape cartridge device so that, in the event of a <u>hard disk</u> <u>crash</u> or comparable failure, the data will not be lost.[79]

TCO – Total Cost of Ownership. An analysis meant to figure out the lifetime costs of expenditures that result from the ownership of certain kinds of assets; these include costs of acquisition, purchase, maintenance, change management, environmental impact, and any other costs that can be reasonably assumed, for any given asset or resource.[99]

technology architectures. The application of IT resources to meet specific business requirements, including determining which IT investments will yield the best return.[12]

technology life cycle. The length of time between a piece of hardware or software's implementation and retirement, measuring the likely effect of that technology on a business product's profitability.[15]

tier one applications. An information system that is vital to the running of an organization. Tier 1 applications include enterprise resource planning and customer relationship management.[69]

unstructured data mining. Searching through and gathering information that is stored in some way other than a row-column database, making the specific data sought more difficult to find; data of this sort include email and word-processing documents, for example.[14]

unused capacity. The amount of potential resources left after factoring in resources that are protective or productive; these are often data storage or processing resources.[3]

variable costs. Expenses that rise and fall according to external factors such as availability of materials, demand for products and services, changing political or environmental constraints, and other possible variables.[21]

virtualized instance. Also called a virtual environment, an isolated environment on a server that has been virtualized to run multiple environments; see virtualization.[84]

virtualization software. (1) Virtualization is software technology that makes it possible to run multiple operating systems and applications on the same server at the same time.[112] (2) Programs that allow you to run multiple operating systems simultaneously on a single computer.[54]

virtual private network. A method using encryption to provide secure access to a remote computer over the Internet.[17]

web application development process. The steps in creating a client-server software application that a client runs in a web-browser, or is run on mobile devices but uses data from the internet; these steps are envisioning the direction of the project, devising a plan, developing the project, and testing.[70]

web content management software. Programs, or systems, (usually web based) that facilitate the creation, management and delivery of information (content and documents), typically via corporate websites, portals, extranets or intranets.[31]

workflow. The series of steps a piece of work passes through from inception to completion; for example, administrative or industrial steps.[120]

Bibliography

[1] AccountingTools.com. (n.d.). "Fixed Cost." Retrieved 13 Aug. 2015 from http://www.accountingtools.com/definition-fixed-cost.

[2] Accounting Tools. (n.d.). "What Are Examples of Operating Expenses?" Retrieved 11 Aug. 2015 from http://www.accountingtools.com/questions-and-answers/what-are-examples-of-operating-expenses.html.

[3] Accounting Tools. (n.d.). "What Is Idle Capacity?" Retrieved 18 Feb. 2013 from http://www.accountingtools.com/questions-and-answers/what-is-idle-capacity.html.

[4] Accounting Tools. (n.d.). "What Is Indirect Overhead?" Retrieved 21 Aug. 2015 from http://www.accountingtools.com/questions-and-answers/what-is-indirect-overhead.html

[5] Apprenda Inc. (n.d.). "Pay-Per-Use Software (SaaS)." Retrieved 17 Aug. 2015 from http://apprenda.com/library/glossary/definition-payperuse-software-saas.

[6] Averkamp, Harold. (2004). "Depreciation Explanation." AccountingCoach.com. Retrieved 14 Aug. 2015 from http://www.accountingcoach.com/depreciation/explanation

[7] Balko, Corey. (2014). "The Difference between Service Catalog and Service Portfolio." Intact Technology Blog HP Elite Software Partner IT

Consulting. Hewlett Packard, 16 Aug. 2014. Retrieved 30 July 2015 from http://www.intact-tech.com/blog/service-portfolio/.

[8] Beal, Vangie. (n.d.). "Agile Software Development." A Technology Definition from Webopedia.com. IT Business Edge. Retrieved 21 Aug. 2015 from http://www.webopedia.com/TERM/A/agile_software_development.html.

[9] Beal, Vangie. (n.d.). "Cloud Management." A Webopedia Definition. IT Business Edge. Retrieved 14 Aug. 2015 from http://www.webopedia.com/TERM/C/cloud_management.html.

[10] Beal, Vangie. (n.d.). "Encryption." A Technology Definition from Webopedia.com. IT Business Edge. Retrieved 21 Aug. 2015 from http://www.webopedia.com/TERM/E/encryption.html.

[11] Beal, Vangie. (n.d.). "ERP - Enterprise Resource Planning." A Technology Definition from Webopedia.com. IT Business Edge. Retrieved 19 Aug. 2015 from http://www.webopedia.com/TERM/E/ERP.html.

[12] Beal, Vangie. (n.d.). "Information Technology (IT) Architect." A Technology Definition from Webopedia.com. IT Business Edge. Retrieved 14 Aug. 2015 from http://www.webopedia.com/TERM/I/information_technology_IT_architect.html.

[13] Beal, Vangie. (n.d.). "SAN - Storage Area Network". A Technology Definition from Webopedia.com. IT Business Edge. Retrieved 21 Aug. 2015 from http://www.webopedia.com/TERM/S/SAN.html.

[14] Beal, Vangie. (n.d.). "Unstructured Data." A Technology Definition from Webopedia.com. IT Business Edge. Retrieved 21 Aug. 2015 from http://www.webopedia.com/TERM/U/unstructured_data.html.

[15] Boundless. (n.d.). "The Technology Life Cycle." Boundless Management. Retrieved 14 Aug. 2015 from https://www.boundless.com/management/textbooks/boundless-management-textbook/organizational-culture-and-innovation-4/technology-and-innovation-37/the-technology-life-cycle-202-3486/.

[16] BrightPlanet.com. (28 June 2012). "Structured vs. Unstructured Data." Retrieved 17 Aug. 2015 from http://www.brightplanet.com/2012/06/structured-vs-unstructured-data/.

[17] Burke, Jon. (June 2015). "What Is Virtual Private Network (VPN)?" SearchEnterpriseWAN. TechTarget. Retrieved 21 Aug. 2015 from http://searchenterprisewan.techtarget.com/definition/virtual-private-network.

[18] Business Continuity Institute. (n.d.). "Business Continuity." Retrieved 17 Aug. 2015 from http://www.thebci.org/index.php/resources/what-is-business-continuity.

[19] BusinessDictionary.com. (n.d.). "Data Management." Web Finance Inc. Retrieved 11 Aug. 2015 from http://www.businessdictionary.com/definition/data-management.html.

[20] BusinessDictionary.com. (n.d.). "Full Time Equivalent (FTE)." WebFinance Inc. Retrieved 21 Aug. 2015 from http://www.businessdictionary.com/definition/full-time-equivalent-FTE.html.

[21] BusinessDictionary.com. (n.d.). "Variable Cost." Web Finance Inc. Retrieved 13 Aug. 2015 from http://www.businessdictionary.com/definition/variable-cost.html.

[22] Carr, Nicholas G. (2008). The Big Switch: Rewiring the World, from Edison to Google. New York: W.W. Norton.

[23] Centre for Addiction and Mental Health (CAMH) Knowledge Exchange. (2 Feb. 2009). "Determine the Service Delivery Model." Retrieved 30 July 2015 from http://knowledgex.camh.net/policy_health/substance_use/mmt_community_guide/Pages/determine_service_delivery_model.aspx.

[24] Chappell, David. (2008). "A Short Introduction to Cloud Platforms". David Chappell & Associates. Retrieved 21 Aug. 2015 from http://davidchappellopinari.blogspot.com/2008/08/short-introduction-to-cloud-platforms.html.

[25] Christensson, Per. "Server Definition." Tech Terms. (16 April 2014). Accessed 14 Aug. 2015. http://techterms.com/definition/server.

[26] Christensson, Per. "Storage Capacity Definition." Tech Terms. (13 Aug. 2009). Accessed 14 Aug. 2015. http://techterms.com/definition/storagecapacity.

[27] CloudTweaks.com. (2 July 2012). "The 4 Primary Cloud Deployment Models." Retrieved 17 Aug. 2015 from http://cloudtweaks.com/2012/07/4-primary-cloud-deployment-models.

[28] Cole, Ben. (Sept. 2014). "Records Retention Schedule." TechTarget.com. Retrieved 21 Aug. 2015 from http://searchcompliance.techtarget.com/definition/Records-retention-schedule.

[29] ComputerWorldUK.com (19 Mar. 2012. "Transition to Cloud - The Journey." Technology Blog and Community from IT Experts. Retrieved 14 Aug. 2015 from http://www.computerworlduk.com/blogs/cloud-vision/transition-to-cloud--the-journey--3570968/.

[30] Ehrens, Tim. (2010). "Customer Relationship Management (CRM)" SearchCRM. TechTarget.com. 2010. Retrieved 19 Aug. 2015 from http://searchcrm.techtarget.com/definition/CRM.

[31] Elcom.com. (n.d.). "Web Content Management Explained in Plain English." Retrieved 21 Aug. 2015 from http://www.elcomcms.com/en-us/resources/articles/wcm_plain-english/wcm_plain-english.

[32] Entrepreneur.com. (n.d.). "Return on Investment (ROI)." Retrieved 13 Aug. 2015 from http://www.entrepreneur.com/encyclopedia/return-on-investment-roi.

[33] Evanna Automation. (n.d.). "Automation Capabilities." Retrieved 17 Aug. 2015 from http://www.evanaautomation.com/automation-capabilities.

[34] Expert Technology Associates. (05 Feb. 2013). "Hosted, Managed or Premise-Based Phone System: Which Is Best for My Business?" Retrieved 14 Aug. 2015 from

http://www.expertta.com/ebulletin/hosted-managed-or-premise-based-phone-system-which-is-best-for-my-business.

[35] Faure, Frederic. (16 Aug. 2010). "Scaling an AWS Infrastructure - Tools and Patterns." HighScalability.com. Retrieved 17 Aug. 2015 from http://highscalability.com/blog/2010/8/16/scaling-an-aws-infrastructure-tools-and-patterns.html.

[36] Frand, Jason. (n.d.). "Data Mining: What Is Data Mining?" UCLA. Retrieved 17 Aug. 2015 from http://www.anderson.ucla.edu/faculty/jason.frand/teacher/technologies/palace/datamining.htm.

[37] GCFLearnFree.org. (n.d.). "Computer Basics: Understanding Operating Systems." Goodwill Community Foundation. Retrieved 17 Aug. 2015 from http://www.gcflearnfree.org/computerbasics/2.

[38] GFI Software. (2010). "On-Premise vs. Cloud-Based Solutions." Microsoft. Retrieved 17 Aug. 2015 from https://www.gfi.com/whitepapers/Hybrid_Technology.pdf.

[39] Gupta, Nitin. (23 Jan. 2013). "CUDA Programming: The Complexity of the Problem is the Simplicity of the Solution." CUDA Programming Blog. Retrieved 17 Aug. 2015 from http://cuda-programming.blogspot.com/.

[40] Hawkins, Jeff. (July 2010). "Data Deduplication (Intelligent Compression or Single-Instance Storage." SearchStorage. TechTarget. Retrieved 21 Aug. 2015 from http://searchstorage.techtarget.com/definition/data-deduplication.

[41] Hurwitz, Judith, and Robin Bloor. (n.d.). "Cloud Computing Delivery Models." For Dummies. John Wiley & Sons. Retrieved 17 Aug. 2015 from http://www.dummies.com/how-to/content/cloud-computing-delivery-models.html.

[42] Informatica Corporation. (n.d.). "Data Integration Hub." Retrieved 21 Aug. 2015 from https://www.informatica.com/products/data-integration/data-integration-hub.html#fbid=1N69DEmde0c.

[43] International Data Corporation (IDC). (n.d.). "World IT Spending by Consumption Model." IDC Worldwide Black Book. Retrieved from https://www.idc.com/getdoc.jsp?containerId=IDC_P336

[44] Interoute.com. (n.d.). "What Is PaaS?" Retrieved 14 Aug. 2015 from http://www.interoute.com/what-paas.

[45] Investopedia.com. (18 Mar. 2008). "Activity-Based Costing (ABC)." Retrieved 11 Aug. 2015 from http://www.investopedia.com/terms/a/abc.asp.

[46] Investopedia.com. (23 Nov. 2003). "Labor Intensive." Retrieved 21 Aug. 2015 from http://www.investopedia.com/terms/l/laborintensive.asp.

[47] Investopedia.com. (24 Nov. 2003). "Outsourcing Definition." Retrieved 11 Aug. 2015 from http://www.investopedia.com/terms/o/outsourcing.asp?adtest=term _page_v14_v1.

[48] Janssen, Cory. (n.d.). "What Are Data Center Operations?" Techopedia. Janalta Interactive Inc. Retrieved 21 Aug. 2015 from https://www.techopedia.com/definition/29871/data-center-operations.

[49] Janssen, Cory. (n.d.). "What Is a Proof of Concept (POC)?" Techopedia. Janalta Interactive Inc. Retrieved 21 Aug. 2015 from https://www.techopedia.com/definition/4066/proof-of-concept-poc.

[50] Jayaram, M. N. (2006). "Capability Maturity Model (CMM)." SearchSoftwareQuality. TechTarget. Retrieved 14 Aug. 2015 from http://searchsoftwarequality.techtarget.com/definition/Capability-Maturity-Model.

[51] JM Bullion.com. (10 Sept. 2014). "Where Do Spot Prices Come From?" Retrieved 19 Aug. 2015 from http://www.jmbullion.com/investing-guide/pricing-payments/spot-prices/.

[52] Koder, Karen. (Apr. 2005). "Footprint?" WhatIs.com. TechTarget. Retrieved 21 Aug. 2015 from http://whatis.techtarget.com/definition/footprint.

[53] Leake, Allan. (17 Mar. 2014). "Database Definition." SearchSQLServer. TechTarget. Retrieved 11 Aug. 2015 from http://searchsqlserver.techtarget.com/definition/database.

[54] Lo, Kevin. (19 Jan. 2011). "Virtualization 101." Tech Soup. Retrieved 30 July 2015 from http://www.techsoup.org/support/articles-and-how-tos/virtualization-101.

[55] Malouf, Laura. (1 July 2010). "Service Catalogs vs. Service Portfolios: What's the Difference?" IT Service Management. Samanage. Retrieved 30 July 2015 from https://blog.samanage.com/it-service-management/service-catalogs-vs-service-portfolios-whats-the-difference/.

[56] Mathias, Craig J. (Oct. 2013). "Identity Management (ID Management)." SearchSecurity. TechTarget. Retrieved 21 Aug. 2015 from http://searchsecurity.techtarget.com/definition/identity-management-ID-management.

[57] Merriam-Webster.com. (n.d.). "Microprocessor." Retrieved 17 Aug. 2015 from http://www.merriam-webster.com/dictionary/microprocessor.

[58] MongoDB.com. (n.d.). "NoSQL Database Explained." Retrieved 5 Oct. 2015 from https://www.mongodb.com/nosql-explained

[59] Mukasey, Michael, Jeffery Sedgewick, and David Hagy. (2008). "Electronic Crime Scene Investigation: A Guide for First Responders (2nd ed.). National Institute of Justice Special Report. Bureau of Justice.

[60] NDB LLP. (n.d.). "SSAE 16 Type II Compliance Audit." The Official SSAE 16 Resource Guide. Retrieved 21 Aug. 2015 from http://www.ssae16.org/important-elements-ssae16/ssae-16-type-ii-compliant.html

[61] Niessink, Frank, Victor Clerc, and Hans Van Vliet. (6 Dec. 2002). "The IT Service Capability Maturity Model." Retrieved 14 Aug. 2015 from www.sysqa.nl/wp-content/uploads/2012/01/IT-service-CMM-1v0.pdf

[62] O'Brien, Russell. (1 Mar. 2008). "Integration Architecture Explained." HubPages. Retrieved 21 Aug. 2015 from

http://russellobrien.hubpages.com/hub/Integration-Architecture-Explained.

[63] OIT Communications Group. (2015). "Definition of Information Security." University of Nevada, Las Vegas. Retrieved 11 Aug. 2015 from http://oit.unlv.edu/network-and-security/definition-information-security.

[64] Open Definition.com. (n.d.). "Guide to Open Data Licensing." Retrieved 14 Aug. 2015 from http://opendefinition.org/guide/data/.

[65] Open Group. The. (n.d.). "Cloud Computing Portability and Interoperability." Retrieved 14 Aug. 2015 from http://www.opengroup.org/cloud/cloud/cloud_iop/cloud_port.htm.

[66] Oracle Corporation. (1 Apr. 2009). "Benefits of Application Rationalization: Reduce Costs and Improve Service with a Systematic Approach." Retrieved 30 July 2015 from www.oracle.com/us/products/applications/042763.pdf.

[67] Oracle Corporation. (n.d.). "Data Warehousing Concepts." Retrieved 21 Aug. 2015 from https://docs.oracle.com/cd/B13789_01/server.101/b10736/concept.htm.

[68] Orenstein, David. (1 Jan. 2000). "Application Programming Interface." Computerworld Inc. Retrieved 21 Aug. 2015 from http://www.computerworld.com/article/2593623/app-development/application-programming-interface.html.

[69] PC Magazine Encyclopedia. (n.d.). "Tier 1 Application Definition from PC Magazine Encyclopedia." Ziff Davis LLC. Retrieved 21 Aug. 2015 from http://www.pcmag.com/encyclopedia/term/66677/tier-1-application.

[70] PC Magazine Encyclopedia. (n.d.). "Web Application Definition from PC Magazine Encyclopedia." Retrieved 21 Aug. 2015 from http://www.pcmag.com/encyclopedia/term/54272/web-application.

[71] Peacock, Mark. (1 Oct. 2009). "IT Service Delivery Model Overview." Archstone Consulting. Retrieved 30 July 2015 from

http://www.slideshare.net/peacock.ma/it-service-delivery-model-overview.

[72] Rawson, Bianca. (Oct. 2013). "What Is Risk Assessment?" SearchCompliance. TechTarget. Retrieved 11 Aug. 2015 from http://searchcompliance.techtarget.com/definition/risk-assessment.

[73] Rouse, Margaret. (n.d.). "Array Definition." SearchStorage. TechTarget. Retrieved 19 Aug. 2015 from http://searchstorage.techtarget.com/definition/array.

[74] Rouse, Margaret. (n.d.). "Cloud Marketplace Definition." Retrieved 05 Oct. 2015 from http://searchcloudprovider.techtarget.com/definition/cloud-marketplace

[75] Rouse, Margaret. (n.d.). "IT Elasticity Definition." SearchCIO. TechTarget. Retrieved 13 Aug. 2015 from http://searchcio.techtarget.com/definition/IT-elasticity.

[76] Rouse, Margaret. (n.d.). "Object-oriented Programming (OOP)" SearchSOA. TechTarget. Retrieved 19 Aug. 2015 from http://searchsoa.techtarget.com/definition/object-oriented-programming.

[77] Rouse, Margaret. (Apr. 2005). "File Sharing Definition." SearchMobileComputing. TechTarget. Retrieved 21 Aug. 2015 from http://searchmobilecomputing.techtarget.com/definition/file-sharing.

[78] Rouse, Margaret. (Sept. 2005). "High Availability (HA) Definition." SearchDataCenter. TechTarget. Retrieved 17 Aug. 2015 from http://searchdatacenter.techtarget.com/definition/high-availability.

[79] Rouse, Margaret. (Sept. 2005). "Tape Backup Definition." SearchStorage. TechTarget. Retrieved 21 Aug. 2015 from http://searchstorage.techtarget.com/definition/tape-backup.

[80] Rouse, Margaret. (Apr. 2006). "Interoperability Definition." SearchSOA. TechTarget, Apr. 2006. Web. 14 Aug. 2015 from http://searchsoa.techtarget.com/definition/interoperability.

[81] Rouse, Margaret. (May 2006). "Business-IT Alignment Definition." WhatIs.com. TechTarget. Retrieved 14 Aug. 2015 from http://whatis.techtarget.com/definition/business-IT-alignment.

[82] Rouse, Margaret. (Oct. 2006). "Bare Metal Environment Definition." SearchServerVirtualization. TechTarget. Retrieved 17 Aug. 2015 from http://searchservervirtualization.techtarget.com/definition/bare-metal-environment.

[83] Rouse, Margaret. (Feb. 2007). "Layer Definition." SearchSoftwareQuality. TechTarget. Retrieved 17 Aug. 2015 from http://searchsoftwarequality.techtarget.com/definition/layer.

[84] Rouse, Margaret. (June 2009). "Server Virtualization Definition." SearchServerVirtualization. TechTarget. Retrieved 21 Aug. 2015 from http://searchservervirtualization.techtarget.com/definition/server-virtualization.

[85] Rouse, Margaret. (Aug. 2010). "Data Archiving Definition." SearchDataBackup. TechTarget. Retrieved 21 Aug. 2015 from http://searchdatabackup.techtarget.com/definition/data-archiving.

[86] Rouse, Margaret. (Aug. 2010), "Hadoop Definition." SearchCloudComputing. TechTarget. Retrieved 21 Aug. 2015 from http://searchcloudcomputing.techtarget.com/definition/Hadoop.

[87] Rouse, Margaret. (Aug. 2010). "On-demand Computing Definition." SearchDataCenter. TechTarget. Retrieved 19 Aug. 2015 from http://searchdatacenter.techtarget.com/definition/on-demand-computing.

[88] Rouse, Margaret. (Aug. 2011). "Recovery Time Objective (RTO) Definition." WhatIs.com. TechTarget. Retrieved 21 Aug. 2015 from http://whatis.techtarget.com/definition/recovery-time-objective-RTO.

[89] Rouse, Margaret. (2012). "Strategic Sourcing Definition." SearchFinancialApplications. TechTarget. Retrieved 14 Aug. 2015 from http://searchfinancialapplications.techtarget.com/definition/strategic-sourcing.

[90] Rouse, Margaret. (1 Feb. 2012). "Data Center Resiliency Definition." SearchDataCenter. WhatIsIt? Retrieved 13 Aug. 2015 from http://searchdatacenter.techtarget.com/definition/resiliency.

[91] Rouse, Margaret. (1 Sept. 2012). "Consumption-based Pricing Model Definition." SearchCloudApplications. TechTarget. Retrieved 13 Aug. 2015 from http://searchcloudapplications.techtarget.com/definition/consumption-based-pricing-model.

[92] Rouse, Margaret. (Sept. 2013). "Cloud Broker Definition." SearchCloudProvider. TechTarget. Retrieved 21 Aug. 2015 from http://searchcloudprovider.techtarget.com/definition/cloud-broker.

[93] Rouse, Margaret. (Aug. 2014). "Multi-tenancy Definition." WhatIs.com. TechTarget. Retrieved 17 Aug. 2015 from http://whatis.techtarget.com/definition/multi-tenancy.

[94] Rouse, Margaret. (2015). "Authentication Definition." SearchSecurity. TechTarget. Retrieved 21 Aug. 2015 from http://searchsecurity.techtarget.com/definition/authentication.

[95] Rouse, Margaret. (Jan. 2015). "Infrastructure as a Service (IaaS) Definition." SearchCloudComputing. TechTarget. Retrieved 14 Aug. 2015 from http://searchcloudcomputing.techtarget.com/definition/Infrastructure-as-a-Service-IaaS.

[96] Rouse, Margaret. (Apr. 2015). "Service-level Agreement (SLA) Definition." SearchITChannel. TechTarget. Retrieved 14 Aug. 2015 from http://searchitchannel.techtarget.com/definition/service-level-agreement.

[97] ScaleDB.com. (n.d.). "Database-as-a-Service (DBaaS)." Retrieved 14 Aug. 2015 from http://www.scaledb.com/dbaas-database-as-a-service.php.

[98] Schedlbauer, Martin. (n.d.). "Making the Business Case for New Opportunities." Corporate Education Group (CEG). Retrieved 21 Aug. 2015 from

http://www.corpedgroup.com/resources/pm/MakingBusinessCase.as
p.

[99] Schmidt, Marty. (08 Aug. 2015). "What Is Total Cost of Ownership
TCO?" Business-Case-Analysis.com. Solution Matrix Ltd. Retrieved 13
Aug. 2015 from https://www.business-case-analysis.com/total-cost-
of-ownership.html.

[100] Schmidt, Marty. (20 Aug. 2015). "What Is Depreciation? Schedules
Defined Accounting Examples Explained." Business-Case-Analysis.com.
Solution Matrix Ltd. Retrieved 21 Aug. 2015 from
https://www.business-case-analysis.com/depreciation.html.

[101] Singleton, Derek. (28 July 2011). "What Is SaaS? 10 Frequently Asked
Questions About Software as a Service." The Software Advice Blog.
Retrieved 14 Aug. 2015 from
http://blog.softwareadvice.com/articles/enterprise/saas-faqs-
1072811/.

[102] SQLCourse.com. (n.d.). "What Is SQL?" IT Business Edge. Retrieved 17
Aug. 2015 from http://www.sqlcourse.com/intro.html.

[103] Stangenelli, Joe. (9 Feb. 2015). "Guide to Virtualization Hypervisors -
Network Computing." Network Computing. Information Week.
Retrieved 30 July 2015 from
http://www.networkcomputing.com/data-centers/guide-to-
virtualization-hypervisors/d/d-id/1318945.

[104] TechCrunch.com. (n.d.). "Why Every Site Should Have a Data
Portability Policy." Retrieved 21 Aug. 2015 from
http://techcrunch.com/2010/06/23/data-portability-policy/.

[105] Techopedia.com. (1 Jan. 2010). "What Is a Mission Critical System?"
Janalta Interactive Inc. Retrieved 13 Aug. 2015 from
https://www.techopedia.com/definition/23583/mission-critical-
system.

[106] University of Alaska. (16 June 2009). "FAQs - Classification | HR
Classification and Compensation." Retrieved 14 Aug. 2015 from
https://www.alaska.edu/classification/

[107] University of North Carolina. (2013). "Information Technology Services: Software Licensing, UNCG." The University of North Carolina, Spring 2013. Retrieved 11 Aug. 2015 from https://its.uncg.edu/Software/Licensing/

[108] Van Fossen, Brita. (Feb. 2015). "Capex (Capital Expenditure)." WhatIs.com. TechTarget. Retrieved 11 Aug. 2015 from http://whatis.techtarget.com/definition/CAPEX-capital-expenditure.

[109] Veracode.com. (02 Feb. 2014). "Software Development Lifecycle (SDLC). Retrieved 17 Aug. 2015 from http://www.veracode.com/security/software-development-lifecycle.

[110] Verizon Wireliess [Online]. "Pay As You Go." Retrieved 19 Aug. 2015 from http://www.verizonwireless.com/prepaid/pay-as-you-go/.

[111] Virtual Geek. (30 Jan. 2014). "Understanding Storage Architecture." Virtual Geek. EMC. Retrieved 21 Aug. 2015 from http://virtualgeek.typepad.com/virtual_geek/2014/01/understanding-storage-architectures.html

[112] VMWare.com. (1 Jan. 2015). "Virtualization." Technology & Virtual Machine Software. Retrieved 30 July 2015 from https://www.vmware.com/virtualization/how-it-works.

[113] Walton, Andy. (1 Jan. 2015). "Electronic Storage Devices & Technology." Chron. Demand Media. Retrieved 30 July 2015 from http://smallbusiness.chron.com/electronic-storage-devices-technology-62349.html.

[114] Waynforth, Chris. (July 2010). "Single Sign-on (SSO) Definition." SearchSecurity. TechTarget. Retrieved 21 Aug. 2015 from http://searchsecurity.techtarget.com/definition/single-sign-on.

[115] WebAssist.com. (n.d.). "Pre-built Web Applications." Instant, Pre-built PHP Websites. Retrieved 21 Aug. 2015 from http://www.webassist.com/web-apps.

[116] Welch, Jack. (18 May 2004). "Change before you have to." Rotterdam School of Management, Erasmus University. Retrieved 6 Oct 2015

from https://www.rsm.nl/about-rsm/news/detail/1315-jack-welch-on-management-change-before-you-have-to

[117] WhatIsCloud.com. (n.d.). "Cloud Deployment Models." Retrieved 05 Oct. 2015 from http://whatiscloud.com/cloud_deployment_models/index

[118] WhatIs.com. (n.d.). "Reference Architecture Definition." TechTarget. Retrieved 21 Aug 2015 from http://whatis.techtarget.com/definition/reference-architecture

[119] WhatIs.com. (n.d.). "What Is Cost Management?" TechTarget. Retrieved 21 Aug. 2015 from http://whatis.techtarget.com/definition/cost-management.

[120] Wulong, Tang. (Oct. 2014). "Workflow Definition." SearchCIO. TechTarget. Retrieved 21 Aug. 2015 from http://searchcio.techtarget.com/definition/workflow.

[121] Zwilling, Martin. (05 Jan. 2011). "Five Smart Exit Strategies." Business Insider. Retrieved 14 Aug. 2015 from http://www.businessinsider.com/startup-exits-should-be-positive-and-planned-early-2011-1.

[122] Zwilling, Martin. (27 Dec. 2010). "Top 10 Product Pricing Models For Startups." Business Insider. Retrieved 17 Aug. 2015 from http://www.businessinsider.com/ten-top-product-pricing-models-for-startups-2010-12.

www.ingramcontent.com/pod-product-compliance
Lightning Source LLC
Chambersburg PA
CBHW071147050326
40689CB00011B/2014